NARCISSISTIC PROCESS AND CORPORATE DECAY

NARCISSISTIC PROCESS AND CORPORATE DECAY

The Theory of the Organization Ideal

Howard S. Schwartz

NEW YORK UNIVERSITY PRESS
New York and London

Copyright © 1990 by New York University
All rights reserved
Manufactured in the United States of America

Library of Congress Cataloging-in-Publication Data

Schwartz, Howard S., 1942–
    Narcissistic process and corporate decay :
    the theory of the organization ideal
    Howard S. Schwartz.
        p. cm.
    Includes bibliographical references (p.   ) and index.
    ISBN 0-8147-7913-1 (acid-free paper) ISBN 0-8147-7938-7 (pbk.)
    1. Corporate culture—United States.
    2. Organizational behavior—United States.
    3. General Motors Corporation—Management.
    4. United States. National Aeronautics and Space Administration—Management.
    5. Challenger (Spacecraft)—Accidents.
    I. Title. HD58.7.S348 1990 302.3'5—dc20 90-13242
                                                    CIP

New York University Press books are printed on acid-free paper,
and their binding materials are chosen for strength and durability.

Book design by Ken Venezio

p 10 9 8 7 6 5 4 3 2 1

For Robbie and Cassie. And for Rebecca.

Fool: Can you make no use of nothing, nuncle?
Lear: Why, no, boy. Nothing can be made out of nothing.

Shakespeare, *King Lear*

Contents

Acknowledgments

My students and friends who have taught me about organizational life have been my most important intellectual benefactors. Since I cannot mention them all by name, it seems to me wise not to mention any of them by name. The thoughts and observations of B. A., B. D., D. S., and P. B. have been especially helpful.

Larry Hirschhorn has become something of an alter ego for me. There are often times when I do not know where my mind stops and his begins. I have an idea that something similar may happen to him. At any rate, such a relationship is not always smooth, so I am grateful to have an opportunity like this to say publicly how much I admire his work and value his friendship.

Howell Baum and Michael Diamond have been my friends, intellectual confederates, traveling companions, and the protectors of my soul. Without their support, I think it would have dried up and blown away.

Harry Levinson gave support for my work when I needed it desperately, and support of the sort that someone can give only when his or her own accomplishment is beyond question. I am very grateful to him.

Chris Argyris, whom I have never met, has generously given my work the benefit of his wisdom, his good sense, and his own unique point of view. My work has benefitted greatly from it and I, personally, have been honored by it.

The International Society for the Psychoanalytic Study of Organizations has been a forum in which I have been able to present my work and learn from the work of others. Democrat though I am, I have to admit that there is something to be said for being a member of an elite. At the least it has given me an opportunity to meet regularly with a number of people who have, each in his or her own way, become very important to me. In addition to Michael, Howell, Larry, and Harry, I would like to mention Leo Gruenfeld, Gilles Amado, Tom Gilmore, Jim Krantz, Michael Hoffman, Laurent Lapierre, Roger Dunbar, Susan Schneider, Larry Gould, and Donald Levine.

One of the real pleasures of working on this book has been the opportunity to work with Kitty Moore. I have dearly appreciated her wonderful combination of good judgment and good cheer.

I would like to thank Leo Goldberger for believing that there was a book to be made out of the jumble I sent him.

My former wife, Katherine Bihm Schwartz, helped me greatly in the course of development that led to this book. She taught me that the purpose of writing was to say what I was thinking and helped me to believe that what I was thinking was worth saying.

Mary Van Sell has, over the last few years, come to be a friend and a person whose judgment I could rely upon in developing my work. I am grateful to have had her as a colleague. I would also like to thank David Doane.

Dan Braunstein, when he was my department chair, did as much as he could, within his constraints, to help me do my work. Liz Barclay, now that she is chair, is doing the same. I think that's worth a word of thanks.

Thanks also to David Garvelink and Dr. Norman Jackson, for doing what they did.

My children, Robbie and Cassie, offered me their wise counsel in choosing the color of the cover of this book. In time, I am sure they will understand that, at the time of year in which this book was published, New York University Press needed all its green and red for Christmas wrapping.

My mother, Hattie Schwartz, and my sister, Susan Anzaha, have invariably loved me. Often they provided for me the only emotional bedrock that I had.

Also, I would like to express my deepest appreciation to the men and women of the fellowship of Alcoholics Anonymous, who have taught me more than I thought I could know.

Finally, I wish to thank the following for granting me permission to quote from copyrighted material:

The New York Times Company for "Design and Tests of Booster . . . ," February 12, 1986; "NASA Admits Cold Affects Shuttle Seal," by Philip M. Boffey, February 12, 1986; "Analyst Who Gave Shuttle Warning . . . ," by Philip M. Boffey, February 14, 1986; "How See-No-Evil Doomed Challenger," by David E. Sanger, June 29, 1986; "NASA Wasted Billions . . . ," by Stuart Diamond, April 23, 1986; "NASA Considered Shuttle Boosters Immune . . . ," by John Noble Wilford,

February 3, 1986; "NASA Officials Say Shuttle Program Had . . . ," by Philip M. Boffey, April 4, 1986; "Inquiry Head Says NASA . . . ," by Philip M. Boffey, February 28, 1986; "Communications Channels at NASA . . . ," by David E. Sanger, February 28, 1986; "Rocket Engineers Tell . . . ," by Philip M. Boffey, February 26, 1986; "Zeal and Fear Mingle . . . ," by Philip M. Boffey, March 17, 1986; "NASA Chief Vows to Fix . . . ," by John Noble Wilford, June 10, 1986. Copyright © 1986 by The New York Times Company. Reprinted by permission.

Farrar, Straus & Giroux and International Creative Management, Inc. for an excerpt from *The Right Stuff* by Tom Wolfe. Copyright © 1979 by Tom Wolfe. Reprinted by permission.

William Morrow & Co. and Acton and Dystel, Inc. for excerpts from *Rude Awakening: The Rise, Fall and Struggle for Recovery of General Motors,* by Maryann Keller. Copyright © 1989 by Maryann Keller.

Random House, Inc. for excerpts from *"I Touch the Future . . .": The Story of Christa McAuliffe,* by Robert T. Hohler. Copyright © 1986 by Robert T. Hohler. Reprinted by permission of Random House, Inc.; for excerpts from *Prescription for Disaster,* by Joseph J. Trento. Reprinted by permission of Crown Publishers, Inc.

Multimedia Product Development, Inc., for excerpts from *On a Clear Day You Can See General Motors: John Z. De Lorean's Look Inside the Automotive Giant,* by J. Patrick Wright. Copyright © 1979 by J. Patrick Wright and reprinted with permission of the author.

The Organizational Behavior Teaching Society for excerpts from "The clockwork or the snakepit: An essay on the meaning of teaching organizational behavior," *Organizational Behavior Teaching Review,* XI (2), 1987, 19–26.

MCB University Press for excerpts from "The symbol of the space shuttle and the degeneration of the American dream," *Journal of Organizational Change Management,* 1 (2), 1988, 5–20.

The Southern Management Association for excerpts from "On the psychodynamics of organizational totalitarianism," *Journal of Management,* 13 (1), 1987, 41–54.

The European Group for Organizational Studies for excerpts from "Antisocial actions of committed organizational participants: An existential psychoanalytic perspective," *Organization Studies,* 8 (4), 1987, 327–40.

ABC News for excerpts of interviews with Senator John Glenn and

Mr. Bruce Murray, broadcast on *This Week with David Brinkley,* June 8, 1986.

Elsevier Science Publishers B. V., Amsterdam, for excerpts from "Organizational disaster and organizational decay: The case of the National Aeronautics and Space Administration," *Industrial Crisis Quarterly,* 3 (4), 1989, 1–16.

The Trustees of Columbia University in the City of New York for excerpts from "On the psychodynamics of organizational disaster: The case of the space shuttle Challenger," *The Columbia Journal of World Business,* XXII (1), Spring 1987, 59–67.

The MacNeil/Lehrer Productions for excerpts of an interview with Dr. Richard Feynman, broadcast on *The MacNeil/Lehrer News Hour,* June 9, 1986.

Part One

THE THEORY OF THE ORGANIZATION IDEAL

Introduction

When I left graduate school and began teaching organizational behavior courses, I was struck by the irrelevance of what I had learned to the actual organizational experience of my students.

My students experienced and understood organizational life as a kind of "vanity fair," in which individuals who were interested in "getting ahead" could do so by playing to the vanity of their superiors. One needed to do this in two ways: one needed to flatter the superior as an individual and as an occupant of the superior role. This latter process tended to trail off into an adulation of the organization in general.

Work either fit into this process of adulation, in which case it made sense; or it did not, in which case it did not make sense. Work that did not make sense in this way, my students felt, was best left to the suckers who hadn't figured out yet how to get ahead and who deserved whatever torment this system led them to inherit. If, through this process, important, valid information was lost to the system by being withheld or simply unappreciated, that was not their concern. Through luck or guile, the consequences would, or could be made to, occur on somebody else's watch.

At first glance, my students' attitude looked to me like cynicism. But closer analysis suggested that, although they had a great deal of cynicism in them, they were not being simply cynical, for they believed in the righteousness of what they were doing.

For them, getting ahead was a moral imperative, which justified any means necessary for its accomplishment. But more than this, the system itself, which called upon subordinates to idealize it, was held morally sacrosanct. A person who refused to go along with the system was seen as not only stupid and naive, but as morally inferior. And this was so even if the individual in question was offering a point of view that was essential for the organization to do its work effectively and efficiently.

It thus seemed to me that, for my students, the organization's processes defined moral value. As defined by its processes, the organization seemed to exist in a moral world of its own, which served to justify anything done on its behalf and which did not require justification on any grounds outside of itself. This view was inconsistent with a view of the organization as an instrument to do work. For my students, the organization did not exist in order to do work; it did work in order to exist.

Yet, even while holding this point of view, many of my students did not appear to have a deep loyalty to the organizations they so supported. On the contrary, for the most part they were willing to change organizations with no regrets or guilt. Their loyalty, if that is what it was, seemed to be to an abstract idea of organization, an idea of the organization as a vehicle for the revelation of their own grandiosity. Ultimately, therefore, their loyalty appeared to be to themselves.

Over time, trying to be a good empiricist, I came to take their stories about organizational life increasingly seriously. I made the assumption that organizational life was just what my students, whom I came to consider my research subjects, and sometimes informants, appeared to be living. Relegating what I had learned in graduate school to the status of a fantasy, I tried to fashion a theoretical conception that would explain this organizational reality.

The theory came to center on the Freudian (1955a, 1957; Chasseguet-Smirgel 1985, 1986) concepts of narcissism and the ego ideal. In this part of the book I try to use these concepts to explain the experience of my students. I do this through an interpretation of the idea of the organization that they hold. The reader will understand, however, that I do not intend just to interpret an idea. For, if I am correct, those who hold this idea of organizations do so in a way that determines their behavior. It therefore provides a basis for the interpretation and understanding of organizational process, insofar as that process is based upon this psychological dynamic.

The vision of organizations I have developed here is negative. Certainly, the topics I have chosen to investigate—totalitarianism, decay, antisocial actions, and so forth—represent parts of the seamy side of organizational life. I make no apologies for this. These matters concern me, and I offer my work as my best attempt at trying to understand them.

The determination as to how much of organizational reality is represented by this vision must be left up to each reader. My own estimate, specifically with regard to American organizations in our epoch, is that a great deal of organization behavior can be understood in this way. And I offer the further hypothesis that the evident inability of American industry to compete may be due, in no small measure, to the dynamics I describe here.

1

The Clockwork or the Snakepit: An Essay on the Meaning of Teaching Organizational Behavior

There is a problem in teaching introductory organizational behavior courses that used to cause me great distress. Most of the textbooks in this area have always seemed to me to be essentially useless for the purpose of teaching students about organizations.[1] Yet the students expected and even demanded that one of these texts be used. For my own part, believing that my purpose was to teach students about organizations and that organizational reality more closely approximates a snakepit than the bland picture most texts convey, I've developed and used a psychoanalytic framework, expressed in this book, that explains much of what I see and have heard about. The problem was that this split my course into two separate courses, almost entirely distinct from one another.

One was the course that I taught. It focused on organizations as they seemed to me to exist in reality. The other was a course, taught by the text, which focused on organizations that seemed to me to exist only in fantasy. This situation was unsatisfactory both to my students and to me.

Trying to resolve this issue, I did an experiment in one of my classes. I first asked my students to form in their minds a picture of the organization they knew best, either from their own experience or from listening to the accounts of somebody close to them. Then I described two types of organizations. One type was a textbook organization. In it, the organization is like a clock: everybody knows what the organization is all about and is concerned solely with carrying out its mission; people are basically happy at their work; the level of anxiety is low; people interact with each other in frictionless, mutually supportive cooperation; and if there are any managerial problems at all, these are basically technical problems, easily solved by someone who has the proper skills and knows the correct techniques of management.

The other type of organization, the "snakepit" organization, is just the opposite of the textbook projection. Here, everything is always falling apart, and people's main activity is to see that it doesn't fall on them; nobody really knows what is going on, though everyone cares about what is going on because there is danger in not knowing; anxiety and stress are constant companions; and people take little pleasure in dealing with each other, doing so primarily to use others for their own purposes or because they cannot avoid being so used themselves. Managerial problems here are experienced as intractable, and managers feel that they have done well if they are able to make it through the day.

Having presented these alternatives, I asked my students to indicate which type of organization more closely approximated the picture of the organization they knew best.

The results were dramatic. Approximately three quarters of the students responded, and, of those, virtually all indicated that the snakepit model fit better. Here was my answer, I thought. The snakepit, each of them knew, was not an exception to the rule; it was the rule. We could forget about the clockwork picture presented by the texts. Organizations aren't like that. So now we could turn to the study of the snakepit with a clear conscience. We were, after all, there to study organizational behavior, right?

Not according to them! For the demonstration, impressive enough to me, had no impact on the bulk of my students. Facts be damned. They wanted to know the techniques for managing clockworks.

For the thinker with clinical interests, the bizarre is the point at which things begin to get interesting. How was it possible to reconcile the interest of my students in the textbook/clockwork image of the organization with the fact that the best evidence of their own senses, and of the senses of their peers, was that such things do not exist?

Over time, I came to believe that the idea of the clockwork organization had much more than pragmatic significance for them. It was rather an article of faith. And, as with all articles of faith, the way to understand this one is to understand its place in the individual's psychological configuration. We hold to articles of faith because we need to. That is why they cannot be dislodged by facts. In other words, the question becomes what did the idea of the clockwork organization mean to these students? What did it represent to them that was so important for them to believe in?

THE CLOCKWORK ORGANIZATION AS AN EGO IDEAL

The idea of the clockwork organization, I propose, symbolized an ego ideal for my students. As we shall see more elaborately later on, it represented the return to narcissism—the healing of the rift between subject and object, self and other, freedom and necessity, that permeates postinfant mental life. It represents the end of the instability in the sense of identity that arises from these (Sartre 1953; Lichtenstein 1977). Under the circumstances, it is not surprising that my students were attached to it. They wanted to know about the clockwork organization not because it represents a perfect organization, but rather because it represents the possibility of becoming perfect themselves.

The problem is, of course, that while the clockwork organization is an idea that has great emotional appeal, it does not represent anything that exists in the world, or even that could possibly exist in the world. It is appealing because students believe that they can redefine themselves in terms of the organization, but in fact all they can do is act the role. There is a qualitative difference here. Defining themselves in terms of the organization would mean defining away what is particular and concrete about them. This is what makes it possible to think of the organization as a clockwork: if everyone in it is defined in terms of the same collective "person," there is no basis for bruising competition, for there is only one person. But what is particular and concrete about one is oneself. We take ourselves with us wherever we go.

The clockwork organization has the same problems connected with it as any ego ideal. The ego ideal is formulated as a response to anxiety, and we are driven to pursue it by anxiety. It represents an end to the anxiety that drives us toward it. But at its core, our anxiety concerns our finitude, vulnerability, and mortality (Becker 1973), and these are the biological givens of being an organism (Freud 1955b). We can transcend biology only in fantasy. The clockwork organization is one of these fantasies.

The fact that we bring our own particularity, finite and vulnerable, to organizational life and the fact that organizational life has no use for that particularity combine to explain, perfectly adequately, the snakepit character of organizational life. For an organization is a drama (Goffman 1959)—a play put on by actors. And there is room in this drama only for the performance. But the performance is put on by a performer, who always differs from the performance. Yet the performance defines us normatively, specifies who we should be. Thus the performer is not what he or she is supposed to be. This means that there must be for each of us, individually and collectively, a shameful, secret underside to organizational life. Where does this leave the teacher of organizational behavior?

Given the premise that organizations are snakepits, it is obvious why one should teach that they are snakepits: because the business of the college professor is to teach the truth. But given the premise that they are snakepits, I can also think of five arguments why one should teach that they are clockworks nonetheless. I don't think that any of these arguments is adequate; but each of them seems inadequate in a sufficiently interesting way to justify refutation.

TEACHING THE CLOCKWORK

The first two arguments propose that one should teach the clockwork theory because students demand it. One of these may be called the consumer-sovereignty argument. Here, the college professor rests the legitimacy of teaching the clockwork model on the basis that he or she is providing a service that students want. There is not much to this argument. It is the equivalent of saying that the physician should make a diagnosis based upon what the patient wants to hear. It countenances, in short, a betrayal of the academic profession. While what it describes might be explainable in some instances, given the necessity of the professor to maintain his or her job, this says nothing more than that universities can be snakepits, too.

The other variant of the argument from student demand is more subtle. I call it the argument from necessary illusion. It recognizes the basically defensive character of the belief in the clockwork organization and asserts a compassionate case for not shattering the student's psychological defenses. The case here is similar to one I experienced in a former incarnation, as a teaching assistant in a humanities program. There, I would lead discussions focusing on the critique of systems of ideas, including philosophies and religions. Every now and then, I would have a student who held the religious beliefs that were under attack. What does one do in a situation like this? If such beliefs give a person solace, is it always good to interfere—especially if one has no equally comforting alternative to offer?

On the level of religious beliefs, it seems to me, this is a most disturbing question. Even Freud (1961), who argued for the abandonment of religion, expressed clear misgivings about his conclusion. On the level of organizational beliefs, the question is less formidable. The difference is that religious beliefs ultimately address the meaning of life, while organizational beliefs refer only to the facts of life. One can live an entire life and maintain belief in religious ideals. Disillusionment with organizational beliefs usually sets in shortly after one gets a job (Klein and Ritti 1984). Under the circumstances, the trade-off becomes the maintenance of a comforting illusion during the student's college life versus the consequences of maladaptation after graduation (Wanous 1975). Add to this the opportunity costs associated with foregoing a veridical education about organizations, and it does not seem to me that the results of the calculation can be in doubt.

At any rate, anyone still concerned about the effects of attacking someone's defenses should bear in mind the experience I had when I was dealing with the issue in the sphere of religion. What I found there was that, despite my horror at what the massive power of my intellect would do to the minds of my poor religious students, I had little reason to worry. Defenses, if that was what they were, defend. These students did not come to their beliefs through reason, and they did not feel much threatened when reason came to attack them. The notion that the intellect is irresistible is perhaps an element of our own narcissism, as teachers, which we would do well to examine on our own behalf.

The third argument for teaching the clockwork strikes me as being the most compelling. It is that the clockwork organization not only is a more appealing picture of organizational life, but represents a better organization. It is, perhaps, not what organizations as we experience them are like, but it is what organizations should be like, and therefore teaching this model might bring organizations closer to the ideal through the actions of our students. I refer to this as the argument from idealism.

The problem with the argument from idealism is that it mistakes the qualitative difference between clockwork and snakepit organizations for a quantitative one. If the difference between the clockwork and the snakepit could be placed upon some continuum, even upon a set of continua, it would make sense to try to approximate the clockwork and to work toward it incrementally. But if the difference is a difference in kind, then no amount of incremental change is going to matter. Thus, if one values longevity, then it makes sense to pursue ways to increase peoples' lifespans. But if it is immortality that one values, then increasing lifespan will be beside the point.

My contention is that the clockwork organization, as an ego ideal, represents an impossible bridging of the gap between the self and the other. The theorists of the clockwork organization want to bridge this gap by proposing the organization as a unity of self and others—a unity created by the redefinition of both selves in terms of organization. But this unity falls apart on the new grounds of being a contradiction between the abstract (the idea of the organization as a unity) and the particular (the individuals who would have to give this abstraction whatever reality it could have). Each of these individuals remains particular, finite, and, hence, separate from the abstraction. But the abstraction is just the idea of the lack of separation. That is what gives it its attractiveness. Thus, the clockwork organization is impossible—a contradiction—and a state that, because of its contradictory nature, cannot even be approximated in a way that would maintain its character as attractive.

The easiest way to miss this point is by supposing that the organization is behavior. Analysis of the ego ideal shows that it is the intentional context of the behavior that poses the problem. I have no doubt that people can behave as if their association functioned like a clock. But within the ego ideal of the clockwork organization is the idea that people are acting spontaneously. And to the extent that people are acting as if the organization were a clockwork, they are not expressing themselves spontaneously. Their experience of their existence as actors would stand apart from, and in contradiction to, the roles they are playing. But this distinction, between the player and the role, is just the contradiction between the individuals and the abstraction that we saw earlier—and that we saw was a fatal flaw in the notion of the clockwork organization.

My penultimate argument is one that I think many teachers of the clockwork theory would find most natural to them. Let me call it the argument from necessity. It holds that the clockwork theory should be taught because organizations will demand it from their employees, and it will be necessary for them to know if they are to get jobs, keep them, and work their way through the hierarchy.

I think there is a good deal of truth to this argument, but not as an argument for teaching the clockwork theory. Rather, it is an argument for teaching the snakepit theory and showing how using the language of the clockwork theory is a strategy for getting by in the snakepit. Unfortunately, this part of the lesson is often only tacit. The teacher teaches the clockwork theory, not with an expression of belief in it or commitment to its truth, but because "I'm supposed to teach you this stuff, so here it is." The student "learns" in a similarly detached fashion, making notes on it and studying it in preparation for an exam. Neither party takes it seriously, and both understand that what they are going through is a kind of charade: the charade of the wise professor who knows the truth and imparts it and of the dutiful, conscientious student who sops this truth up and comes to know it and to revere the teacher who teaches it. In other words, what we have here is a perfect lesson in the way the theory of the clockwork is used in the snakepit.

The pity is that, to the extent that this lesson remains tacit, to the extent that the participants pretend to take the clockwork theory seriously, a great deal of pedagogical leverage is lost. The teacher loses the opportunity to discuss the importance of vanity in the organization, to consider the place of meaningless rituals that serve only to separate the powerful from the powerless, to address the way language can be used to avoid communication rather than create it, and to face the loneliness and isolation that must result. In short, the teacher loses the opportunity to confront with the students many of the very facts that make snakepits snakepits.

There is one further argument that needs to be considered here. Not precisely an argument for the clockwork theory, it may still be seen as a variant of the clockwork theory in that it calls for the replacement of the snakepit by a clockwork. I think of this as the argument from self-consciousness. Thus, authors like Argyris and Schön (1974) and Culbert and McDonough (1980), who have done brilliant work in developing the theory of the snakepit, suggest that knowing about the snakepit and what causes it can lead organizational participants to an understanding of new ways of organizing that would avoid the traps that lead to the snakepit. They envision new organizational forms that would permit the same union of subject and object that we saw characteristic of the clockwork organization, although on a far more sophisticated level and with much richer notions of the nature of the individual and of his or her relationship to the organization.

Thus, Argyris and Schön (1974) find the problems of organizational life to be the results of participants using a strategy that they call the "Model I theory-in-use," which, if I am not oversimplifying to the point of distortion, consists at least partly in the idea that the way to get something is to try to get it. They want to replace this with the idea that the way to get what you want is to pursue it collaboratively. But, clearly, this works only if those with whom you are collaborating want you to have what you want and are interested in working for you to have it. Thus, an abstract unity of self and other is assumed, which leads us immediately back to the idea of the organization as ego ideal and all the contradictions that involves.

Similarly, Culbert and McDonough (1980) propose an organizational form in which participants understand that everyone has "alignments" —ways of integrating their own interests with the requirements of the organization—and in which others' alignments are respected by every- one. This envisions the contradictory union of one's own identity, in which one's own alignment has unique significance by virtue of its being one's own alignment, with an organizational identity, in which one's own alignment has no special place but is simply one organizational alignment among many. This organizational form is, again, an abstract unity of self and other—an ego ideal.

TEACHING THE SNAKEPIT

There are many arguments for the clockwork theory, even though none of them is adequate. I can think of only two for teaching the snakepit, but I think they are both compelling.

The first argument is really an argument against teaching the clock- work. It may be called the argument from negative consequences. Let us suppose that the teacher managed to teach the clockwork picture so successfully that the conception survived the student's disillusionment with his or her work experience. What would be the consequences? As I shall discuss more fully in later chapters, it seems to me that the student would most likely feel that, since his or her experience does not match up with the ego ideal, there must be a deficiency on his or her own part or in his or her situation. Since the ego ideal is the person one is supposed to be, a deficiency on one's own part will be experienced as shameful (Piers and Singer 1953). On the other hand, if the belief in the clockwork is to be maintained, it must be believed that there are others who are more what the organization really is and who are the ego ideal. These would typically be seen as those higher up in the organization. Thus, the belief in the clockwork may lead to an experience of the delegitimation of the individual vis-à-vis those higher in the hierarchy.

Now let us look at the issue by focusing on those higher up. Suppose that they also were our students and they still believe in the clockwork. The difference between them and those lower down is that they have power. And if the situation they find themselves in is not the clockwork, they can use that power to compel the dramatization of the clockwork they desire and expect. They can, in other words, use their power to enforce the playing out of their own return to narcissism by those over whom they have power. This perspective, combined with that of the individuals lower down who experience delegitimation as part of their own need to maintain belief in the clockwork, forms, then, a picture of tyranny, on the one hand, and of slavishness, passivity, loneliness, and isolation on the other. In a word, as we shall see in the next chapter, this is totalitarianism.

Of course, it goes without saying that, given the appeal of the ego ideal, people can believe in the clockwork without their professors' having taught them to do so. Nonetheless, I should not leave this point without noting the irony that, while all organizations may be snakepits, the theory of the clockwork may be instrumental in causing some to be more snakepittish than others.

The second argument for teaching the snakepit is one to which I alluded earlier. It seems to me so straightforward that it would be egregious to give it a name. It is that organizations are snakepits and that the college professor's work consists in teaching the truth. My view is that this course of action does not lead to any more despair than reality holds in store anyway. What is necessary to pursue it is a certain trust and a certain love. The trust is that one's students will have the moral substance to act responsibly, at the margin, even though they may not believe it will get them into heaven. The love is the basis for that trust.

2

On the Psychodynamics of Organizational Totalitarianism

Understandably, discussions of totalitarianism tend to focus upon its more dramatic manifestations. Unfortunately, this often leads us to miss aspects of totalitarianism that pervade our own times and culture and that may be, if not equally destructive, at least sufficiently destructive to require study and criticism. An exception is the work of Earl Shorris (1981) on totalitarian aspects of corporate life.

Shorris defines *totalitarianism* as the process of defining people's happiness for them. The element that makes this process noxious is that the definer of happiness is not the person whose happiness is being defined. This has the effect of taking the individual's sense of determining the direction of his or her life away from that individual and ceding it to another, whereas it is the very sense of giving direction to our lives, even if only in thought, that constitutes our moral autonomy. For Shorris, who in this respect echoes George Herbert Mead's (1934) distinction between the *I* and the *me,* the human being stands apart from any symbol. It is this standing-apartness that constitutes one's self-consciousness, that is the source of one's specific identity. To cause a person to collapse into a symbol one has projected for him or her is to cause the self-consciousness to become, not the essence of that person's identity, but something alien to it—to separate the person from him- or herself.

This is the fundamental psychodynamic of totalitarianism. It alienates people from themselves and gives them over to others. Whatever victories may ensue must be pyrrhic. Whatever happiness is to be attained here is not the happiness of the individual. Indeed, it is not happiness at all. It is the drama of happiness attaching to a role that the person performs in a play that is written and directed by others.

We can gain insight into the underlying psychodynamics of this process by exploring the connection between Shorris's view and the Freudian theory of narcissism and the ego ideal, which we began to explore in chapter 1.

NARCISSISM AND THE EGO IDEAL

For Freud (1957) the infant starts off in the congenial state of being at the center of a loving world. To add a bit to what we saw in the previous chapter, it is thus a perfect combination of agency and communion, subjectivity and objectivity, activity and passivity, freedom and determinateness, yang and yin. Freud refers to this happy synthesis as "primary narcissism."

But the world is, alas, not a loving place, and none of us are the center of it. No one in it loves us quite as much as we need to be loved. And if, as life goes on, others are to love us at all, we must love them in return—and give up, in a word, the centrality that the love of others was an instrument for preserving. Further, even if I gain the love of a few individuals, what good does it do me? My real problem is with the world. And they cannot protect me from it any more than I can protect them. For the world can do very well without me. It did without me before I was and it will do without me when I am not. In the end, by virtue of the laws of biology if nothing else, I get rubbed out. To be sure, I can make some contribution to the world. Perhaps, in some sense, that will live after me. But what is it that lives after me? Obviously, whatever it is, it is not me. The world is precisely the arrangement that, among other things, this shall happen. Why should I love that? If I don't, what ground is there for my making any contribution to the world at all?

The idea that the world was not made with us in mind, that the only place we can have in it is small and temporary, underlies what Melanie Klein (1975) called the "depressive position." You can understand why. Much of the psychology of social institutions is organized against this position.

For Klein, the depression of the depressive position is often defended against by adopting what she calls the "manic defense," or a regression to an earlier stage of development called the "paranoid-schizoid position." The characteristic psychology here is determined by what she calls "splitting," which is a lack of integration of the good aspects of the world with the bad aspects and a denial of the ultimate reality of the bad aspects. In one way or another, we attribute the cause of our anxiety to a person or a place or a time or a group or a social arrangement or a part of ourselves and direct our aggression at this "bad" stuff. We hold before us the image of a perfect "good" world that will be our world when the bad stuff is gotten rid of or gotten away from.

This good world represents for us the possibility of a return to narcissism, to a world in which annihilation is not a problem, a world in which it is perfectly all right to do whatever we want to do, a world that has us as its reason for being, a world free of anxiety. Stories of the goodness of the good world and stories of the roots of our anxiety constitute mythology and help structure culture. A main function of culture, that is to say, is to give content and direction, to render sensible, our longings to return to narcissism and to avoid the anxiety arising from our mortality (Becker 1971, 1973).

In Freudian terms, the representation that we make to ourselves of the good world is what I have been referring to as the ego ideal. This is what we are driven toward by our anxiety over our finitude, by our rejection of whatever it is about ourselves that is vulnerable and limited. Because this is our spontaneous self, it is always the case that the motivation toward the ego ideal involves the rejection (in Freudian terms, the repression) of our spontaneity, our "real self" (Horney 1950). Thus, we experience the pursuit of the ego ideal as an imperative—as an attempt to be what we ought to be, not a natural expression of what we are. The recognition that we are not what we are supposed to be, that we are playing a role rather than being the role we are playing, is the experience of shame (Goffman 1959). Another consequence, as we saw before, is that we never get to be the ego ideal. The ego ideal represents us as we believe we would be if we could get rid of what causes our anxiety. But what causes our anxiety is what is most specifically ourselves. While we are alive, we can never get rid of it—it is one's own individual life.

As Freud (1955a) pointed out, the ego ideal may be formed in any of a number of ways. Of particular interest in this book is the case in which an abstraction, a leading idea, has taken the place of a leader, and in which that abstraction is the idea of the organization itself. In this case, we may recognize the committed organizational participant as a person whose ego ideal is the organization.[1] Thus, for the committed organizational participant, the organization represents a means for the return to narcissism.

To talk about the organization as ego ideal is not to refer to the actual organization but to the committed person's idea of the organization, which may have little relation to the person's experience with the actual organization. It is what the committed organizational participant holds out as what the organization is supposed to be and would be except for the effect of "bad" aspects of the world, and what he or she accepts as an obligation to help bring about. This is clearly an ideal organization. Indeed, I refer to this concept, that of the organization's serving the function of the ego ideal, as the *organization ideal*. How does the organization ideal serve as an ego ideal, and what are the consequences?

THE EGO IDEAL AND THE ORGANIZATION IDEAL

In the first place, the organization ideal represents power. Denhardt (1981) has noted how deeply the concept of control is built into our concept of the organization. In psychoanalytic terms, the organization ideal serves as a reaction formation that covers over and represses the anxiety-evoking idea of our finitude, vulnerability, and mortality (Schwartz 1982, 1985; Diamond 1984).

Second, the organization ideal is a scenario of love as well and offers the possibility of a return to centrality in a loving world. For, by taking the organization as ego ideal, the individual assumes the possibility of a boundary-dispelling relationship to others who have done likewise. Both love and centrality are possible in this scenario, because each of the individuals who have taken the organization as their ego ideal assumes that the others have also redefined themselves as the organization and therefore as essentially the same and having the same interest. Conflict is defined away, therefore, and along with it all social anxiety within the organization. Indeed, what we have here is a perfect analog for Freud's reference to the tale of Narcissus, who falls in love with his own image in a pond. Here, the other organizational participants would ideally provide a mirror for the focal participant and reflect that participant's love for her- or himself.

Third, a related point ties the intrapsychic processes involved to the normative structure of the organization. We have seen that, by defining themselves in terms of the organization, individuals put themselves into an interesting relationship with others who have done the same: on the one hand, this is a relationship of idealized love that would not interfere with narcissism; on the other hand, it is a relationship of mutual responsibility because it is up to each to uphold the organization ideal for all the others. It becomes not only a matter of the fulfillment of mutual personal principle but the direct object of moral sanction—the threat of the loss of love—by ideally loved others. This gives a moral force to the maintenance of the definition of oneself and one's relations as the organization ideal.

Fourth, and perhaps most comprehensively, defining oneself as the organization removes from consideration a problem that in a way contributed most powerfully to the anxiety the participant was trying to allay. As noted before, the self-conscious self, the spontaneous self, Mead's (1934) *I*, though it is on the one hand what is most intimately myself, is also the cause of my greatest ontological trouble. For it can never be fully represented by a symbol (Mead's *me*) and therefore cannot become part of the enacted world, but always stands aside from my enactments and says of them, "That is not me, that is not me." Defining myself as the organization ideal solves this problem for me. Having defined myself in terms of the organization as an ethical standard, I have a basis upon which I can reject my spontaneous self-consciousness as an obstacle to my self and to my obligations. It becomes an impulse for me to negate: a source of shame and guilt. What I cannot deny phenomenologically, I can repudiate morally. To be sure, I can do that only by rejecting that part of me that is most uniquely myself. But after all, it was precisely the fact that I have a spontaneous self that got me into trouble in the first place.

To illustrate, consider an interview that Studs Terkel (1974) conducted with a man named Wheeler Stanley, who was then the youngest general supervisor in a Ford assembly plant. From an impoverished background, Stanley had come, through Ford, to a position of status in the world and felt that he was in line for more. His ambitions lay within the company hierarchy, and his conscious concerns were company concerns. His ego ideal was the organization ideal. But listen to the way this conversation evolved:

I've got a great feeling for Ford because it's been good to me. . . . My son, he's only six years old and I've taken him through the plant. . . . And that's all he talks about: "I'm going to work for Ford too." And I say, "Oh, no you ain't." And my wife will shut me up and she'll say, "Why not?" Then I think to myself, "Why not? It's been good to me." (185)

Stanley here expressed an underlying resentment at Ford, which was not acceptable to his moral consciousness. He reported an occasion when the veneer slipped and the thought was blurted out. But then it was repudiated as unworthy, and the veneer of the company man was put back in place. "[Ford] has been good to me," replaced and covered over the apparently spontaneous opposite thought: "Ford has been bad to me."

Fifth, the repudiation of the spontaneous self leaves open a possibility of a redefinition of the self that is wholly in accordance with the organization ideal. This is a redefinition of the "wants" of the individual. In terms of the organization ideal, the participant undertakes to "want" to do what the organization needs doing. Thus, the polarity of subject and object, activity and passivity, is projected to be overcome.

The picture of the organization as organization ideal will be familiar to all teachers of organizational behavior. This is an organization in which everyone knows what he or she is doing, in which there is no conflict or coercion, in which communication is open and direct, in which people want to do what needs to be done, in which every member is solely concerned with and works diligently to promote the common good. As I argued in chapter 1, the picture is of an organization that has never existed and never will. But somehow it is of the utmost importance to students to be able to believe in it.

Indeed, the picture of the organization as ego ideal is familiar and important not only to the naive observer, but to the sophisticated one as well. The idea of the model organization as the integration of individual spontaneity and organizational necessity is, after all, in one form or another at the heart of many normative theories of organization, and the attainment of the organization ideal is a large part of the promise made by practitioners of "organizational development."

Often, as with Argyris (1957), organizational development efforts are aimed at encouraging what Maslow (1970) called *self-actualization* through work. But notice here that an important shift takes place away from Maslow's concept.[2] Instead of saying that self-actualization means "Be healthy and then you may trust your impulses" (179), these thinkers seem to believe it means "Want what the organization wants you to want, and then you may do what you want."

To this point, we have considered the nature of the organization ideal and its relation to the individual who adopts it as his or her ego ideal. But though the organizational processes so characterized may resemble totalitarianism, they also resemble social processes that are, arguably,

not only more benign, but often even positive, such as idealistic move-
ments for social change. Indeed, these processes involve the psychodynamic underpinnings of social organization generally, at least to the
extent that people put their faith in it. If I have noted that it involves
repression and decentering of the self, I have said no more than Freud in
Civilization and Its Discontents (1961). And if the impossibility of attaining the ego ideal leads almost inevitably to disillusionment, it is at
least arguable that disillusionment is a necessary element of adult development and growth (Levinson 1978). In order to show how the processes I have described lead to totalitarianism, it will be necessary to
show how they tend to degenerate in the context of organizational
power.

HIERARCHY AND ONTOLOGICAL DIFFERENTIATION

Because the organization ideal represents the return to narcissism and
because the return to narcissism can never be achieved, there must be
some way of accounting for the failure of the return to narcissism while
still remaining true to the idea of the organization ideal.

For the committed organizational participant, there are two available
reasons why narcissism has not returned—why I still feel threatened,
why everybody doesn't love me, why I am not doing what I want, and
so on. One possibility involves scapegoating. Here, the anxiety is attributed to "bad" forces, external or internal, that are threatening the
organization. Once the forces can be given an identity, it is possible to
struggle against them. The community of strugglers can be conceived as
wholly good, because all the anxiety can be attributed to the enemy.
Under the circumstances, a quite satisfying degree of localized collective
narcissism can be achieved. This, apparently, represents the dynamic of
the cohesiveness of many in-groups that feel themselves arrayed against
out-groups. We can easily see in it the root of the loyalty, cohesiveness,
and high morale of work organizations that can identify some external
threat or of parts of work organizations that can attribute the organization's problems to other parts of the same organization.

Scapegoating is certainly a tool used by totalitarian work organizations to increase their control. Thus, the president of a major auto
manufacturing company referred to the Japanese as "the enemy" in an
address to Oakland University students. He made it manifest that this

climate of warfare was very much a part of the cultural process underlying his organization's "quality of working life" program. Certainly the feeling of threat from an enemy increases the level of anxiety and therefore the need to believe that the organization is the organization ideal. But the feeling of being threatened by an outside enemy does not, by itself, create the kind of internal split, the alienation, the separation from the self, that totalitarianism represents. In order to account for that, another dynamic must be considered.

This other dynamic involves what I shall call the process of *ontological differentiation*. Here the attribution of the cause of anxiety is made to the self and experienced as shame—shame for oneself and for the parts of the organization with which one is associated. Because the organization is understood as the organization ideal, and because one and one's associates fall short of this ideal, these have evidently not been fully integrated into the organization. One experiences shame as a result of contrasting oneself and one's associates to others who are, one believes, what they are supposed to be—who are more integrated with the organization ideal and presumably do not have the deficiency in their identity that one is ashamed of. This contrast is ontological differentiation.

In the classic bureaucratic organization, ontological differentiation takes the structural form of vertical differentiation, or hierarchy. As Arendt (1966) and Shorris (1981) note, what I am calling ontological differentiation does not always correspond precisely with the organizational pyramid. Arendt, for example, compares the totalitarian organization to an onion, in which one goes deeper and deeper, rather than higher and higher.[3] Thus, the Nazi party, for example, contained ideological fanatics at all levels of the state apparatus, trusted to wield power even over their nominal superiors through their capacity for denunciation. Nonetheless, as Shorris notes, the pyramid and the onion intersect at the point that is both highest and deepest. In traditional organizational terms, this is the top of the organization. For the purposes of this discussion, the dimensions of vertical differentiation and depth will be taken to be combined in the organization's hierarchy.

In the traditional view, hierarchy serves a variety of managerial functions, such as coordination, control, and the like. Although there is certainly some truth to this view, it cannot provide fully for a phenomenology of hierarchy—for the simple reason that hierarchy represents not only a differentiation of function and task, but a moral differentiation as well (Parsons 1954). Thus, the organizational ladder is conceived as a sort of "great chain of being." It represents, in a world, a structured adaptation to the idea that organizational participation does not amount to a return to narcissism, while retaining the idea of the organization as organization ideal, and therefore permitting the idea of the return to narcissism as a possibility.

Thus, it is easy to suppose that more status in the organization's hierarchy will represent a greater degree of attainment of the organization ideal and therefore progress in the return to narcissism.[4] On the one hand, the organization's actions will be more the result of my actions, and its deliberations will include my thoughts. On the other hand, by definition, my actions and thoughts will be the appropriate actions and thoughts with regard to the organization. The problem is that commitment to the belief that progress in the hierarchy will mean progress in the attainment of the organization ideal for me, involves commitment to the belief that it represents such progress for others as well.

Ontological differentiation is the primary vehicle through which organizational and specifically corporate life becomes totalitarian. For at this point it becomes possible for some to use their ontological stature and the power that goes with it to narcissistically impose their fantasy of their own perfection upon others as the organization ideal—or, in Shorris's definition of totalitarianism, for some to define the happiness of others.

The point is that the top of the organization is not merely an abstract position, but has a population and a history of action. *In organizational totalitarianism the organization, as defined by its leadership's understanding of their own actions, is proclaimed to be the organization ideal; and the organization's power is used to impose this as the ego ideal for the organization's participants.*

Thus, locating the return to narcissism at the head of the organization means more than establishing a direction toward the ego ideal. It involves establishing certain definite others, with their own way of looking at the world and at themselves and with their own history of actions, as already ideal. It involves, in other words, acquiescing to the perfection of some specific others as one's own moral obligation, collectively enforceable by all others who have done so and with whom one defines oneself as ideally in community. It legitimizes the coercion by the powerful that causes the less powerful to act out a drama whose theme is the perfection of the powerful. And it does so in such a way that the powerful can feel self-righteous about this coercion—as if they were performing a service or committing a sacrifice.

TOTALITARIANISM AND ONTOLOGICAL DIFFERENTIATION

The human consequences of ontological differentiation can be explored in any of a number of ways. One way is through consideration of the ways in which people's defenses work. It has become a commonplace of cognitive psychology that persons see the world in ways that are systematically biased. Weiner et al. (1971), for example, note a self-enhancing bias that consists of seeing oneself responsible for positive outcomes and others responsible for negative outcomes. The self-enhancement that this bias promotes is the attributional correlate of narcissism.

Now, consider the vicissitudes of this bias in the structure I have described. Here, because the head of the organization serves as the specification of the organization ideal and hence as the definer of reality, we may expect that the reality so defined will have the leader's self-enhancing bias built into it. In terms of maintaining the stability of the organization ideal, this is necessary, but consider the consequences for the subordinate. The subordinate has to see the world in a way that enhances, not his or her own self-image, but the self-image of the leader.

The self-enhancing bias that operates within the subordinate must be abandoned and overruled in favor of the self-enhancing bias of the leader. But whereas the self-enhancing bias of the leader arises naturally and almost automatically in the mind of the leader, for the subordinate to approximate the leader's self-enhancing bias must be a tortuous, contrived, painful, and self-destructive process. And yet the organization ideal demands just that. It demands, in a word, that in the name of the common good, the individual must not only deny his or her own natural tendencies toward self-enhancement and even self-protection, but morally condemn them. Moreover, informal pressure on the part of other participants and even legitimized formal coercion on the part of authorities may be used to enforce this self-abasement. This, it seems to me, is the source of the slavishness and passivity Shorris, for example, finds so common in totalitarianism.[5]

A related feature of totalitarian life is uncertainty regarding the appropriate. If the definition of the appropriate is based retrospectively on the actions and self-definitions of the leader, the subordinate must be in constant uncertainty as to what actions will correspond to the leader's whims. If the rationale of the leader's whims is not comprehended, the result must be not only uncertainty with regard to appropriate action, but uncertainty over one's own moral worth. This is because one's own perceptions, instincts, and analyses cannot be relied upon as grounds for moral judgment and because actions that turn out later to be deviations from the leader's position are condemnable. This is liable to be all the more so to the extent that the subordinate maintains the organization ideal and therefore cannot blame what he or she sees as inadequacies on the organization, but rather has to accept him- or herself as the source of the blame. The result of this must be a more or less permanent state of shamefulness.

The alternative here is cynicism. Remember that the leader is defined as the ideal, rather than having that capacity in reality. The wisdom of the leader's actions and thoughts are limited in just the same way that the rest of ours are. Accordingly, rationality cannot be used as a guide to action on the part of the subordinate. Rather, the particular irrationality that the leader manifests must be the criterion. But a person's specific irrationality, we may suppose, is an outgrowth of that particular person's personality. Although it may come naturally to him or her, it must seem to others, if they understand it at all, as some sort of systematic quirkiness. Understanding this quirkiness, the subordinate may well be able to anticipate the leader's judgments and use this knowledge as a way of "playing the game." The problem is that this can only be achieved through giving up idealization of the organization ideal while, at the same time, one's self-presentation conforms to it. This is cynicism.

Another feature of totalitarianism is the isolation of people from one another. This isolation is related to a similar dynamic. The organization ideal is held in place not only by the subordinate's own need to do what he or she feels ought to be done, but by sanctions issuing from ideally loved others. This means that deviations from them threaten the meaning structures of others whose love is needed to maintain one's own meaning structure.

There is something not only unnatural but positively impossible about becoming someone else. But this is obligatory. The result is that the person one really is not only is unacceptable to oneself, but is unacceptable in social life, which is in turn composed of persons who are each unacceptable in social life for the same reasons. The result is that social interaction takes place not between persons, but between performances. Roles utter words at other roles. And if at any time any one of them were to say, as each of them somehow knows, "This is a bunch of nonsense," that person would become a pariah because he or she would bring out in all these people the anxiety that motivated the performance in the first place and maintained it at all times. Thus, each of these persons must live in more or less complete isolation and be terribly lonely.

An example may be useful to illustrate some of these processes. Some colleagues were doing consulting work for a corporation that was getting ready to open a new plant in our area. A distinguished professor, call him D, well known for his organizational development work, was to give a presentation to the "design team," made up of middle managers recruited from the rest of the corporation, to help them in designing a compensation system for the new plant. I wangled an invitation.

The presentation turned out to be mostly a summary of D's widely published work, spiced with anecdotes about the utopian bliss in the factories he had "installed." As the day went on, I shifted my interest from D's presentation to the response of the design team. I eavesdropped on their informal conversations and watched their body language. Particularly suggestive was the way they responded when it appeared that their leader was going to ask them a question. They looked for all the world like unprepared schoolchildren trying to make themselves inconspicuous so the teacher would not notice them.

It became increasingly clear to me that this was the first time the members of the design team had ever been exposed to systematic thinking about compensation systems. Aside from various idiosyncratic attitudes toward certain aspects of what D was saying, none of them had any thoughts on the matter at all. Moreover, they appeared to know that they were in over their heads. Behind a certain bluster in their facade, I thought I could detect shamefulness and panic. Evidently, this state was not a unique response to this particular subject. A colleague who had been sitting in on the meetings where they "designed" other "behavioral systems" reported that, despite tremendous time investment, very little headway was ever made. From my colleague's account, it appeared that the meetings were consumed by attempts to assign blame for their lack of progress.

These team members had apparently been recruited into what they thought was a fast-track position in a new direction the corporation was taking. Elements of the corporate personnel and training staffs, led by a guru who was officially a "consultant," had managed to persuade the corporate hierarchy to give them wide-ranging control over the design of the new plant, which would employ a new culture, based upon a team concept. So, naturally, a team was recruited to do the design work, with the guru acting as "facilitator." Something magical was supposed to happen when a number of people got together in a room. Each was supposed to contribute him- or herself, and the synergism of their cooperation would add up to a whole that was greater than the parts.

As it turned out, it was not themselves that they were contributing at all. What they had to do, instead, once they were committed, was to figure out what the guru thought the selves were that they were supposed to be, perform those selves, and hope for the best. Their future was out of their own hands and in the hands of the guru. The best the group could do (the hidden agenda, really) was simply to take D's package and adopt it. But they would not be able to admit that they were doing this, because they were supposed to be the "design team" and to fit D's "recommendations" into their own conceptual framework. For the same reason, they couldn't even admit that the "facilitator" was in fact running the show. For the show that the guru was running was one in which they were autonomous, self-determining agents.

The point is that it was the guru's fantasy that was being enacted here. We can imagine that he saw himself as the shepherd loved by his flock, the Lone Ranger who makes factories and travels on, the Taoist sage who moves others without moving himself, perhaps even the revolutionary in the pin-striped suit.

There is no place in any of these for the design team members as the persons that they were. Their function was to be absorbed into the guru's fantasy. Even the promise of the fast track, by which they were enticed, must have been felt as shameful in the fantasy they undertook to enact. No self-serving fantasy can fit into an organization designed around somebody else's narcissism. To be sure, one could come back and say that no narcissistic fantasy has a place in an organization—even the guru's. But that would be naive. For what we mean when we conceive of a perfect organization is an organization ideal; and an organization ideal is a narcissistic fantasy. The only question is who ultimately gets to be the narcissist.

In this case none of them got to be the narcissist. Not even the guru. The company did not build the plant. All of the design team members were laid off. I don't know where the guru is. He is probably pursuing his dream someplace else. And he has another line in his resume.

Finally, perhaps the most poignant loss suffered by participants in organizations of this sort is the loss of the sense of worth and human connectedness that could otherwise come from work. For organizations of this sort do not exist to do useful work. They do work in order to exist. And because their existence is the fiction of their organizational ideal, we may say that everything that goes on within them finds its meaning in connection with maintaining this fiction.

One of my students invited me after class one night to have a drink. One drink turned to many, and I soon was involved in a very sad story of the mortification of a soul that bore upon many of the points I have described here. He was employed by a large corporation in a unit whose function had almost ceased to exist. Yet his supervisor spent all his time trying to expand his empire by hiring more people. What my student did all day, when he did anything at all, was to play up to the vanity of his supervisor and tell him and others how important the supervisor and the department were. He had to do this because he hated it there and wanted a transfer, which required the blessing of the supervisor. The heart of the dilemma turned out to be that the more he was successful at building up the supervisor's image, the more the supervisor refused to permit him to transfer, because the department was, according to the drama, already short on personnel. I asked him why he hated this so much, what he would do if he could do whatever he wanted to at work. He said: "I'm an engineer. All I want to do is build cars."

CONCLUDING REFLECTION

This last observation, that totalitarianism may deprive organizational participants of the opportunity to do useful work, suggests that there is a practical dimension to this issue. It appears that, in the totalitarian organization, productive work comes to be less important than the maintenance of narcissistic fantasy. This cannot help but have an impact on the productivity of the entire enterprise. For totalitarianism represents a turning away from reality. And organizations need to deal with real environments, even if this only means that they need to deal with narcissism projects that are not represented by the organization's own organization ideal. As I shall show below in part 2, such turning away from reality must have serious consequences for the organization's effectiveness.

3

Antisocial Actions of Committed Organizational Participants

In the movie *Silkwood*, a managerial employee of a nuclear chemical corporation is observed by Karen Silkwood as he retouches the photographs of welds in fuel rods intended for nuclear reactors. The man is evidently a committed organizational participant, concerned about the effects on the company and its employees of late delivery on a contract. He does not appear to be a loathsome, evil creature, and yet, the activity he is engaged in is not only illegal; it is potentially destructive in an order of magnitude that is sickening to contemplate. The question that I wish to address in this chapter is how this man and others like him—loyal, moral, and dedicated within the context of their organizational lives—can, in the context of their work, engage in actions that are morally reprehensible.

The answer I will propose goes to the very root of the connection between the individual and the organization, in the sense that it concerns the way in which the organization influences the individual's moral orientation toward the world, and hence the individual's voluntary social action. What we shall see is that a work organization can form its own moral community, that it can form that community on the basis of commitment, that commitment can itself be explained on the basis of a function that participants require organizations to serve, and that the morality of a community so formed can easily stand in isolation from, and even opposition to, the broader community in which it exists and with which it interacts.

When the individual's moral community becomes limited to the work organization, the psychological significance of work can change. From an exchange relationship between workers who produce a product or service and consumers who use it and pay for it, work can come to be experienced as an internal process within the organization—an exchange between the organization and its employees. Understood in terms of this internal process, transactions between producers and consumers can take on an indifferent and even a hostile affective coloration. Under these psychological conditions, the relations of an organization with its environment, including the work that it does, can become exploitative, manipulative, and often even aggressive.

To explain the concept of organizational commitment, I define the *ontological function,* by which I mean the organization's function of providing a sense of identity to its participants. While this idea is certainly not a new one in organizational thought, what I wish to suggest here is why this function is required, what its psychology is, and what it means. For in understanding these features, we will be able to understand how the ontological function, an apparently beneficial phenomenon, and the organizational commitment that results from it, can turn sour and malignant and can lead to the most terrible consequences.

WHY THE ONTOLOGICAL FUNCTION IS REQUIRED

The crucial step in the analysis of the ontological function is to ask the question why is it required? The answer has to be that in many cases, as Lichtenstein (1977) has pointed out, people's sense of identity is tenuous in the extreme.

This seems absurd. How can a person's sense of identity be tenuous? Are not people what they are? Is that not their identity? The answer is that, for the most part, people are not what they are, or, what is the same thing, cannot permit themselves to be what they are.

Thus, it makes sense to say: "He has made something of himself," or "She has become somebody." What we have to notice about these expressions is the implication that, if the persons in question had allowed themselves to be what they were before they became something or somebody, they would not have been anything or anybody. They would not, that is to say, have had an identity. This is to say that having an identity, at least in our culture, is something of an achievement. Again, we have the notion of the "has been," of somebody who once was somebody, but is no longer anybody.

Taking these things together, we find that having an identity is not something we can take for granted. On the contrary, it is something we must achieve if we are to have it at all, and we must continue to achieve if we are to maintain it. In other words, having an identity is a status that is always in question.

Moreover, there is clearly a judgmental element in these assertions. Making something of oneself is good; not making something of oneself is bad. Being somebody is good; being a "has been" is bad. Thus, the question of identity reflects acceptance or rejection, affirmation or denial. Finally, it seems at least plausible that if these sorts of judgments are common when we judge others, something similar probably goes on when we assess and consider ourselves. We have the possibility not only of denying identity to others, but of denying it to ourselves. Indeed, the question of our own identity would, like the question of the identity of others, be continually in question at all times. Never, apparently, can we simply permit ourselves to be simply what we are.

Not allowing ourselves to be what we are just because that is what we are means that we cannot take ourselves as the measure of what we are supposed to be. We look outside ourselves to find out who we are supposed to be, if we are going to be anything at all—if we are going to have an identity. I submit that we fashion social institutions largely to provide an answer to this question. In this way, social institutions, and specifically work organizations, develop an ontological function. To pursue this issue, it is necessary to consider why people are not what they are or cannot permit themselves to be what they are.

THE EXISTENTIAL PSYCHOANALYTIC PSYCHOLOGY OF THE ONTOLOGICAL FUNCTION

To understand that people cannot permit themselves to be what they are is to recognize that at our psychological base lies self-rejection. In order to understand this self-rejection, we must come to an understanding of where and when it originates as a stable part of the psychological structure.

In psychoanalytic theory, self-rejection is not a component of our original psychological configuration. On the contrary, to begin with, the infant experiences itself without any self-critical sense whatever.

The response of others who are oriented toward the child gives the child a sense of importance. Moreover, the child's love of these "mirroring" others, its opening itself to them, allows it to bask in their love for it and to experience that love as love for itself (Lichtenstein 1977).

But while love for others permits self-love, it is also the lever by which self-rejection enters into the child's mental configuration. For as time goes on and as the child comes to enter into more complex relations with its parents and with the world, certain spontaneous actions on the part of the child become unacceptable to the parents and to others generally, and the child's love for them, its openness to them, and its need for their love lead to its experiencing their rejection as self-caused rejection, and therefore as self-rejection.

Thus, in the course of coming to live with others, bringing them into our minds as the "internal objects" (Klein 1975) with whom the meaning of our lives is transacted, we internalize their rejection of us as our rejection of ourselves, which, in turn, forms a stable part of our psychological configuration. In this way, a permanent wound to our narcissism is created. Thus we cannot permit ourselves to be what we are. The locus of our identity shifts from who we are to who others will permit us to be, and the need for the ontological function is developed.

The ontological function refers to the projection of the ego ideal, to the possibility of a return to narcissism, which in this connection means regaining a stable, self-contained identity without self-rejection at its core. It refers to a specification of that person who will be able to be exactly who he or she is and will not be required, under penalty of rejection, to be someone else. We may now observe that the ontological function of the organization consists in specifying an organization ideal to serve as an ego ideal for organizational participants.

Up to this point, there is no problem. All that I have described is benign. There is no way yet to understand why a person would commit criminal and antisocial acts because of concern for the corporation. In order to understand how that can happen, we need to go more fully into the psychology of the ego ideal and organization ideal.

We saw before that self-rejection arises from the internalization of the rejection of loved others. But if this were all that it amounted to, then we could imagine that the return to narcissism could be a real possibility. If one pleases the loved others, they will love one in return, and one will again be the center of a loving world.

There are two problems here. The first, which we saw before in chapter 2, is that orienting oneself toward pleasing others in order to gain their love already means that one is not the center of their world. Rather, those whose love one organizes one's life around are the center of one's own. By orienting my life around their love I am conceding my dependence on them and conceding the fact that they do not, and I cannot make them, love me for myself alone. Rather, if they are to love me, they will love me out of motives arising from within themselves. Accepting that one cannot have ontological hegemony over the world, that in order to have the love of others one must limit one's claims and one's sense of self-importance, amounts to self-rejection.

Thus, if the organization ideal is to succeed in avoiding self-rejection, it must be based upon a redefinition of the self and of others in a way that denies the differences among us—that defines us as being essentially the same and having the same motives and the same center. This denies organizational participants the status of being separate individuals, independent others. Thus, the denial of the possibility of being rejected by others is based upon the fantastical denial that other individuals exist.

The second problem is that, even if I give up centrality in an attempt to gain love, the outcome must ultimately be disillusioning. For ultimately, it is the facts of biology that determine that the world is not a loving place, and the love of loved others, early in life, served to conceal this fact. The point is that the threat of loss of love on the part of the apparently omnipotent parents is experienced so powerfully partly because it reveals to the infant how vulnerable, finite, and, ultimately, mortal it is; and vulnerability, finitude, and mortality remain facts. In other words, the loss of love establishes for the infant that its narcissism was an illusion. This revelation may be repressed, but it can never be eliminated as a basic element of the psychological configuration. I think we can see from this where another part of our internalized self-rejection comes from. It consists in the rejection of the vulnerability, finitude, and mortality that go along with one's organic identity. Thus, the ego ideal and the organization ideal ultimately symbolize immortality. Again we can see why the ego ideal, and the organization ideal along with it, can never be achieved.

ORGANIZATIONAL ASPECTS OF THE ONTOLOGICAL FUNCTION

The phrase *organizational commitment* can now be defined in a way that is consistent with its usage in traditional organizational psychology (e.g., Schein 1983; Mowday, Porter, and Steers 1982) as the situation in which a person's identity is specified by the organization's ontological function. It describes a person, in other words, whose ego ideal is the organization ideal. The question then becomes, how, in the context of organizational activity, is it possible to explain morally reprehensible actions on the part of organizationally committed individuals?

Three features of the ontological function interact to permit this explanation. They are: (a) the content of the organization ideal, (b) the relationship of the individual to the organization ideal, and (c) defense of the identity through defense of the organization ideal.

Content of the Organization Ideal

In the case of the work organization, the content of the organization ideal must first be social—that is to say, it must be an image of social interaction among individual ego ideals, relating to each other in frictionless, mutually supportive, job-specific interaction. This amounts to the requirement, mentioned earlier, that the members of the organization have redefined themselves in terms of the organization and therefore as essentially identical. Second, the ideal must be powerful—in the sense that the individuals, as organized, are rational, know what they are doing, and are competent to do what they are doing and in control of the situation. This would be a presupposition of the possibility of the organization being immortal and therefore providing immortality for those individuals redefined in terms of it. And third, it must be free of anxiety at the level of identity. That is to say, the individuals involved would have to be conceived as performing their organizational roles, not out of a feeling of obligation or compulsion, so as to avoid internal or external rejection, but out of desire or self-expression—not out of lack, but out of plenitude. This would be the equivalent of specifying that the two mentioned causes of anxiety, the existence of separate others and mortality, have been overcome.

Relationship of the Individual to the Organization Ideal

As we saw before, humans never reach the ego ideal. This is also true for the organization ideal. Organizations never reach the organization ideal. That would imply frictionless interaction among totally competent, perfectly rational individuals acting purely out of desire. As we have seen above, this is not a real possibility. The organization ideal would also be an organization not only living in perfect coexistence with its environment, but assured of the permanent continuity of this coexistence. This would imply that the organization would be able to perfectly predict and perfectly control the future and be in total permanent control of its environment. But a godlike organization of this sort cannot be put together with human stuff. These possibilities are not in keeping with reality. They deny human limitation. We can believe them to be possible only because we need to believe it.

Thus, the ontological function essentially requires the creation of illusion. Obviously, this illusion, if it is going to serve its purpose, must be taken as a fact. Accordingly, the ontological function of the organization must also involve the shielding of the illusion from reality, the maintenance of the illusion as an apparent fact in the face of its illusory character. It is this dual process—the creation of illusion and the preservation of the apparent facticity of the illusion—that leads to the malignant consequences I wish to explain.

Committed organizational participants, who require that the organization specify an identity for them, are precisely those who have the need to take these illusions as fact and to shield them from reality. In order to maintain the sense of the organization as organization ideal, they are thus likely to feel that deviations from the organization ideal are the result of their failure to fulfill the conditions of their identity. Ironically, maintaining their fantasy of becoming their "idealized" selves means despising their "actual" selves (Horney 1950). The affect that goes along with this is shame.

Baum (1987) has pointed out the pervasiveness of the feeling of shame among organizational participants. He has observed that superiors can invoke shame among their subordinates simply by doing their job. Another point regarding the relationship of individuals to the organization ideal concerns the necessity of defending the illusion of the organization ideal from being revealed as an illusion in order to maintain the ontological function. This implies that while committed organizational participants believe that their lapse from the organization ideal is a failure on their own part, they may believe that others fulfill the organization ideal.

An important feature of organizational phenomenology in this connection is the experience of hierarchy. As we have seen in chapter 2 (also see Schwartz 1987), it is possible to reconcile individual failure, and even the failure of one's associates, to measure up to the organization ideal through the belief that, at higher levels of the organization, people do approach the organization ideal. Indeed, a large part of organizational dramaturgy is devoted to the enactment of the presumed competence and goodness of organizational superiors (Klein and Ritti 1984).

Defense of Identity through Defense of the Organization Ideal

It is clear enough that, to the extent that the individual is committed and derives his or her identity from the ontological process, that identity is put into question by threats to the organization's existence. Thus, threats to the organization are experienced as threats to the individual. Defense of the organization becomes self-defense. More interesting is that, since the organization ideal is an ideal, threats to the organization are perceived as having a hostile coloration, as aggression, as bad. Defense of the organization may be experienced as a righteous and virtuous action, therefore, regardless of the light in which such action may be seen by the organization's environment—which is seen, after all, as the source of the aggression. Indeed, recalling that the organization is seen as the organization ideal, we may note that it is not only real threats to the organization that are seen as acts of aggression. Even mere threats to the image of the organization as perfect can be seen as reprehensible.

EXPLAINING ANTISOCIAL ACTIONS OF COMMITTED PARTICIPANTS

Taken together, the content of the organization ideal, the relationship of the individual to the organization ideal, and the defense of identity through defense of the organization ideal give an adequate theoretical base for understanding how committed organizational participants can engage in illegal and antisocial acts.

First, and most obvious, the interaction of belief in the ideal character of the organization with feelings of shame over one's own failure to fulfill the organization ideal can lead to the sort of malignant obedience to authority investigated by Milgram (1963). Feelings of shame over failing to meet the ego ideal lead to a moral delegitimation of the self and its natural responses. One is, after all, not what one is supposed to be, and therefore one's spontaneous responses should not be taken as the determinants of one's action. On top of that, higher authority is what it is supposed to be, and therefore its directives are experienced as morally enhanced and more credible as moral directives than the individual's own moral feelings.

But while this process surely explains some antisocial activity on the part of committed participants, it does not explain all of it. Specifically, it does not explain the actions of those who gave the orders, and, generally, it does not explain self-directed antisocial action, such as the retouching of photographs by the employee in *Silkwood*.

The key to understanding self-directed antisocial actions lies in the phenomenology of the individual who experiences threat to the organization as threat to his or her own identity. Since individuals never reach the ego ideal, identity is always in question; and since the organization itself falls short of the organization ideal, in the sense of being less in control of its circumstances than its own mythology requires, the precarious conditions that all organizations continually face may be interpreted as the result of unfair, hostile, and aggressive acts on the part of outside forces—which must be playing unfairly, after all, since the organization is the organization ideal and is therefore doing everything properly and correctly. Under the circumstances, the committed individual may feel that the moral response is one of hostility and aggression (Alford 1990).

In order to get a more rounded perspective on what this antisocial action amounts to, it may be useful to consider the relationship between the organization and its environment. The organization serves, through the committed individual's belief in the organization ideal, an immortality function for the individual (Schwartz 1985). It is, in effect, an instrument for the denial of the individual's finitude. And, in order to fulfill this function, it must itself be considered to be immortal. As we have seen, the individual denies his or her mortality by defining him- or herself as part of an organization that is conceived to be in perfect, permanent control of its environment. But organizations are subject to the same question of identity as individuals are. They are never perfectly in control of their environments. Nor, it is important to note, should they be.

The point is that from a system perspective, the environment can claim a legitimate right to make demands upon the organization. The environment is, after all, where everyone who is not a committed organizational participant exists and has such identity as he or she can manage to have. From the point of view of the environment, the organization is a source of goods and/or services. It is in exchange for the supply of these goods and/or services that the environment provides resources that permit the organization to continue. When the organization fails to provide such goods and/or services as the environment deems sufficient to balance its investment of resources, the environment responds by withholding resources and thereby threatens the survival of the organization. What's wrong with that?

When work is viewed as one side of an exchange relationship between producer and consumer, it always makes sense, in evaluating an organization, to ask what is it good for? What does the organization do for its environment that makes it worthwhile for the environment to keep it in existence at a cost to itself? But this question is not asked by committed organizational participants. For them, the criterion of worth is defined not by the environment but by the organization. Indeed, the criterion of worth is the organization ideal.

Thus, what appear from an extraorganizational perspective to be legitimate demands that the environment places on the organization, appear from the standpoint of the committed participant to be illegitimate, hostile, and aggressive challenges to the organization's and the individual's existence. When I referred before to the need of the committed participant to believe that the organization controls its environment, I was putting the matter too mildly.

In fact, *committed participants cannot tolerate the organization's having an independent environment at all.* From this individual's standpoint, the environment is ontologically linked to the organization, in that its meaning is a function of the organization's needs and agenda. Thus, rather than the organization existing and justifying itself by fulfilling needs of the environment, the environment is thought to exist in order to admire and attend to the organization.

Earlier, we saw that the ego ideal symbolizes the return to narcissism. Now we can see how the organization ideal does so as well. Just as the narcissistic child expects the world to revolve around it, so the organizationally committed individual expects the world to revolve around the organization, conceived as the organizational ideal. Moreover, just as the infant responds with rage when the world does not respond to its whims, so the committed participant may respond with self-righteous, hostile, aggressive, and even criminal activity when the world does not respond to the whims of the organization.

From the standpoint of the broader social world, therefore, antisocial actions are by no means to be regarded as an aberration from normal

organizational activity on the part of organizationally committed participants. On the contrary, they appear to be a natural concommitant of
organizational commitment itself. "Evil," Hobbes said, "is a robust
child" (cited in Becker 1975). I might add, and for the very same reason,
that it can also be a robust organization.

ORGANIZATIONAL COMMITMENT AND ANTISOCIAL
SOCIALIZATION

That antisocial organizational behavior is a concommitant of organizational commitment, which itself would seem to be related to organizational effectiveness and perhaps social usefulness, raises the question of
the circumstances under which such behavior might take place. While
this is properly a question for further research, it does seem possible to
use previous work on organizational commitment and socialization to
provide a basis for informed speculation and for establishing possible
directions for research.

For present purposes I shall restrict myself to a previously mentioned
work by Schein (1983), which I think provides some very interesting
clues. Schein says:

One mechanism [for building commitment] is to invest much effort and time in
the new member and thereby build up expectations of being repaid by loyalty,
hard work, and rapid learning. Another mechanism is to get the new member to
make a series of small behavioral commitments which can only be justified by
him through the acceptance and incorporation of company values. He then
becomes the agent of his own socialization. Both mechanisms involve the subtle
manipulation of guilt. (195)

Going beyond the case of the new recruit to the general case of the
organization participant who has been selected for special treatment and
putting this matter in terms of the ego ideal, it seems to me this passage
is suggesting that selected participants will most strongly take the organization ideal as their ego ideal when (1) the organization succeeds in
presenting itself as an organization ideal, (2) progress toward this organization ideal seems probable for the individual in question, and (3)
other possibilities for the ego ideal have been eliminated. It further
suggests that guilt is involved both in the attraction toward the organization ideal and in the elimination of alternatives. The influence of guilt
(or shame, as we shall see) may provide a key to the whole process.

Take the guilt involved in the presentation and accessibility of the organization ideal. The organization lavishes resources on participants, indicating to them that if they take the organization as an organization ideal, the hierarchical route to that ideal is open to them. The participants, if they are to think themselves worthy of these resources and of the promise of more to come, "must repay the company with loyalty and hard work," as Schein says; the participant "would feel guilty if he did not" (195).

The crucial question to ask at this point is, where do these resources really come from? The answer can only be that they come from the environment. Proximal control over them may rest with the organization, to be sure. But ultimately, of course, they must originate outside the organization. The organization can be no more than a steward for these resources. Accordingly, such a relationship of guilt as may exist would have to be caused by an unbalanced exchange relationship between the participant and the environment, the producer and the consumer. Thus, it appears that the first step in the process through which organizational commitment comes to develop antisocial potentialities is through an obscuring, on the part of the organization, of the source of the resources it employs.

We can see this obscuration in Schein's observation that the organization builds up "expectations of being repaid by loyalty, hard work, and rapid learning." We can see where hard work and rapid learning go into balancing the exchange relationship between participant and environment, but loyalty to the organization? The point to be noted here is that, in the most fundamental sense with regard to the exchange relationship of work, the organization is not a party in the transaction. The organization, strictly speaking, is simply a patterning of this very complex relationship. This is at least one meaning that can be given to Karl Weick's (1969) observation that the organization does not exist; only the process of organizing does. Thus, bringing the organization in as the main party in the transaction is already an act of obscuration.

How is this obscuration possible? Through the same process, I suggest, by which the organization comes to present itself as an organizational ideal. The organization, as a process, once had a positive effect on its environment; and the environment, eager to have the relationship continue, bestowed upon the process an attribution of identity, of causal centrality, and entrusted the constructed entity with the resources it now commands. It made the organization independent. Thus, the environment relinquished proximal control over these resources out of the very admiration and idealization of the organization that make it attractive to the individual rising in its ranks.

In doing so, however, it gave up the means of control that it possessed to require the organization to repay the environment for the resources it had given over. It trusted that the organization would accept the moral responsibility to balance the exchange relationship—that it would undertake an obligation. But if the organization denies the obligation, if it makes the narcissistic claim that the environment should revolve around it, rather than accepting its own moral responsibility to the environment, the environment, by virtue of having made the organization independent, is left without recourse. The environment's rejection of the organization comes to lack meaning.

In asserting its control over the participant's guilt, the organization asserts its right to end it and asserts that it, itself, is free of guilt. Implicitly, it claims it is free of the obligation toward others in the environment that the phenomenology of guilt contains. In other words, it presents itself as being beyond, as transcending, guilt and obligation. It presents itself as a morally independent identity.

By offering to absolve the participant of guilt in exchange for loyalty, the organization creates a self-fulfilling proposition. For loyalty is the acceptance of the organization as one's ego ideal. By this act one does, after all, believe that one is getting away from one's moral dependence on others and over the necessity of being concerned about their rejection —in the terms used earlier, one believes one is creating for oneself an identity that will be beyond question. Thus, the commission of the psychic act of giving the organizational loyalty that, from one's own point of view, provides identity, is the very self-deception, the obscuration, that cuts the organization morally loose from its environment.

Now take the technique of getting behavioral commitments. One example Schein uses is the brainwashing practice of forcing public confession from a prisoner. Another is the act of enticing a rebellious individual to accept a promotion. In both cases, what we see is a behavior that invokes shame among one's prior reference group, as a violation of its own ego ideal—a shame that can only be avoided by rejecting the previous reference group as a source of potential admiration, restricting oneself to the organization ideal, and limiting the circle of one's identifications to those who also have taken the organization ideal as their ego ideal. Then, what would otherwise be seen as shameful actions come to be viewed as signs of commitment and highly valued. This has the effect of refreezing the participant's identity into the organization's meaning system and, effectively, of isolating that meaning system from its environment.

Given that actions, no matter how shameful they look to the environment, may be looked upon as worthwhile within the organization; and given that by presenting itself as an organization ideal the organization obscures the moral relationship that exists between participant and environment, it is clear that anything has become possible. Repeating the point made earlier, that identity so defined is threatened by the very existence of an independent environment, it appears that it is only circumstances that prevent the possible from becoming probable.

CONCLUSION

These last considerations show how the potentiality for antisocial actions is built right into the process of the socialization for organizational commitment. They also show how precisely those organizations that had a favorable response from their environments are most likely to build up the sort of commitment that may lead to antisocial actions when the favor begins to slip. This second point has to be a cause for pessimism, since it implies both that (1) nothing is stable about the kind of identity that commitment to an "excellent" (Peters and Waterman 1982) organization offers, and that (2) there is no way of dealing with this problem in programmatic, institutional fashion, since any institution that was successful in dealing with it would itself be subject to this process of degeneration.

Moreover, there is no cause for optimism in the idea that the solitary individual may be able to withstand the organization's blandishments and maintain a strong moral sense. For, while some rare individuals will do so, many will not. It is, of course, the organization that selects those individuals upon whom it will shower resources and who it will raise to positions of power, expecting commitment in return. Then the solitary individual becomes a deviant, and there is no necessity in this work to repeat what we know about how groups deal with deviants. Look at what happened to Karen Silkwood.

All in all, there is not much cause for optimism in any of the considerations adduced in this chapter. But, then, it is the demand that all of our stories have happy endings that leads to these dynamics in the first place.

Part Two

ORGANIZATIONAL DECAY AND ORGANIZATIONAL DISASTER

Introduction

My first understanding of narcissistic process, organizational totalitarianism, and the organization ideal was in moral terms, in terms of the psychological damage done to the individuals involved and in terms of the damage that could be wrought outside of the organization. But as time went by, it became more and more clear to me that the processes I was coming to understand must have practical consequences as well— consequences for the effective functioning, the efficiency, the profitability, and the competitiveness of organizations. In a word, it did not seem to me that organizations as I understood them could possibly be successful even in terms of the narrowest economic criteria, without regard to the moral costs involved. So, when American industry seemed incapable of competing with foreign enterprises, I did not find myself at all surprised; and when the space shuttle *Challenger* blew up, I thought I knew where to look for an explanation. The next three chapters are attempts to show some of the effects of narcissistic process and totalitarian management on organizational functioning.

I give the name *organizational decay* to the multidimensional degeneration that results when the nature of the organization shifts from doing work in the real world to presenting a dramatization of its own perfection in a fantasy world. Chapters 4 and 5 provide illustrations of organizations in the process of decay. Chapter 4 is a case study of General Motors. Chapters 5 and 6 deal with the National Aeronautics and Space Administration and the *Challenger* disaster. Chapter 5 shows how NASA decayed through the years into an organization that could make the decision that led to the *Challenger* disaster. Chapter 6 discusses the specific decision-making process that launched the *Challenger.*

Chapter 4 makes extensive use of the only account that I know of by a highly positioned corporate insider who became alienated from the system and reported on its processes to the outside. This is a book by John Z. De Lorean, cowritten by J. Patrick Wright, and published by the latter under his own name, called *On a Clear Day You Can See General Motors* (1979).

There are two problems with using De Lorean's testimony. One is that the separation of any individual from an organization renders that person's critical testimony suspect. People tend, often correctly, to see his or her criticism as the defensive reaction of an individual who has been rejected and who "couldn't make it" in the system. De Lorean was, however, "making it" very well, with regard to outward signs, when his separation from GM occurred. As group executive for the Car and Truck Group he was responsible for the core of GM's business, and it was widely believed that he would succeed to GM's presidency.

The other problem is more serious. It is that De Lorean's activity after leaving General Motors was not suggestive of a man whose probity as a witness could be taken without skepticism. His operation of the auto company he created appeared wild and irresponsible, and his involvement in a cocaine deal, even though he was not convicted, did nothing to recommend him as a moral authority.

I am using his testimony with some reluctance, therefore, but I am using it nonetheless, for a number of reasons. First, I have never encountered anyone who disagreed with the facts of De Lorean's claims. On the contrary, these are often taken for granted by people who revile De Lorean himself. Second, all of the evidence I have come to be aware of that bears upon De Lorean's story, however fragmentary, has been supportive. Moreover, his observations and analyses seem to be consistent with a more recent account of GM by Maryann Keller (1989), an account that bears none of his taint. I will be using her work to lend secondary support to my case. Third, and most important, is that De Lorean's account helps one to make sense of GM's current situation.

The fact is that GM is widely believed to be in a state of free-fall. For example, an article in the 14 December 1989 *Wall Street Journal,* headlined *"Losing the Race:* With Its Market Share Sliding, GM Scrambles to Avoid a Calamity," observes that:

GM's 10-year slide in U.S. car-market share is accelerating at an alarming and dangerous rate. It took six years, from 1980 to 1986, for GM's market share to decline five percentage points, to 41% from 46%. Since then, it has taken just three years for GM's share to plunge another six points, to just under 35% so far this year.

And, the article adds:

Market share isn't just a statistic on a board-room chart. And the decline in GM's market share is "absolutely horrifying," says John A. Casesa, automotive analyst at Wertheim Schroeder & Co. in New York. "What's happening now has long term implications. GM's share erosion is a sign that the fundamental problems haven't been fixed." (Ingrassia and White 1989: 1)

If the kind of "fundamental problems" these analysts point to were the processes of organizational decay that De Lorean describes, we could easily understand not only the state GM currently finds itself in, but why it would be so difficult for it to get itself out of it.

4

Totalitarian Management and Organizational Decay: The Case of General Motors

In the most basic sense, organizational totalitarianism places falsehood right at the core of organizational functioning and therefore cannot help but lead to a loss of rationality. As I have noted before, the return to narcissism is impossible, short of psychosis, and therefore organizational totalitarianism means the superimposition of a psychosis upon organizational functioning. Ultimately, such a loss of rationality leads to generalized and systemic organizational ineffectiveness.

Moreover, I suggest that this condition of generalized and systemic ineffectiveness has a unity to it and therefore represents something like an organizational disease. I would like to give it the name *organizational decay*, with the intention of conveying the impression of both an internal process of rot, not occasioned by outside forces, and a holistic process, not taking place in isolated parts of the organization but typically and increasingly sapping the vitality of the organization as a whole. This decay eventually may manifest itself in any of a number of ways. I shall discuss a few of them, relying on De Lorean's book to provide illustrations.

SOME CAUSES OF DECAY

Commitment to Bad Decisions

Perhaps the most obvious symptom of organizational decay is the commitment to bad decisions. Staw (1980) has noted that the tendency to justify past actions can be a powerful motivation behind organizational behavior and can often run counter to rationality. As he observes, the justification process leads to escalating commitment. When mistaken actions cannot be seen as mistaken actions, the principle on which they are made is not seen as being mistaken. Worse, the feeling that it is a valid principle becomes enhanced through the need to defend the decision, and thus further decisions are made on the basis of it.

This process must be especially lethal in the case of the totalitarian organization, where the idea of the perfection of the organization provides the organization's very motivational base. Here, the assumption of the identity of the individual decision-maker and his or her organizational role turns the tendency to justify past actions from a defensive tendency on the part of individuals to a core organizational process—a central element of the organization's culture.

It will be useful here to differentiate between totalitarian management and idealistic or "transformational" (Burns 1978) leadership.[1] Idealistic leadership involves belief in the organization as an organization ideal, but it relies upon a vision of the future that is honestly held and promulgated by the leaders. When the organization catches up with the consequences of its actions and finds them importantly at variance with its earlier idealistic intentions and projections—when it comes to know, in other words, that a decision was a bad decision—it has the choice of either acknowledging its failure, and hence its deviation from the ideal, or of denying its failure and attempting to maintain the image of itself as ideal through deception and compulsion. In the former case, it is possible that through imagination and creativity a revised ideal can be formulated. Even if it is not, the organization will at least have learned something. In the latter case, the organization turns toward totalitarianism.

The case of the Corvair illustrates the process of commitment to bad decisions. Modeled after the Porsche, the Corvair was powered by a rear engine and had an independent, swing-axle suspension system. According to De Lorean, any car so powered and so suspended is going to have serious problems—problems that were well known and documented by GM's engineering staff long before the Corvair was offered for sale. Understanding the significance of the following commentary requires attending to the time it took to reverse the original bad decision.

> The questionable safety of the car caused a massive internal fight among GM's engineers. . . . On one side of the argument was Chevrolet's then General Manager, Ed Cole. . . . On the other side was a wide assortment of top-flight engineers. . . .
>
> . . . One top corporate engineer told me that he showed his test results to Cole but by then, he said, "Cole's mind was made up."
>
> . . . Management not only went along with Cole, it also told dissenters in effect to "stop these objections. Get on the team, or you can find someplace else to work." The ill fated Corvair was launched in *the fall of 1959.*

The results were disastrous. . . .

It was only a couple of years or so before GM's legal department was inundated with lawsuits over the car. . . .

When [Bunkie] Knudsen took over the reins of Chevrolet *in 1961,* he insisted that he be given corporate authorization [to fix the problem with a stabilizer bar, which would have cost $15 a car]. But his request was refused by [top management] as "too expensive."

[Ultimately, under threat of his resignation, they relented.] Bunkie put a stabilizer bar on the Corvair *in the 1964 models.* . . .

To date, millions of dollars have been spent in legal expenses and out-of-court settlements in compensation for those killed or maimed in the Corvair. The corporation steadfastly defends the car's safety, despite the internal engineering records which indicated it was not safe, and the ghastly toll in deaths and injury it recorded. (65–67, emphasis added)

Advancement of Participants Who Detach Themselves from Reality and Discouragement of Reality-Oriented Participants Who Are Committed to Their Work

When core organizational process becomes the dramatization of the organization and its high officials as ideal, the evaluation of individuals for promotion and even for continued inclusion comes to be made on the basis of how much they contribute to this dramatization. This means that increasingly promotion criteria shift from achievement and competence to ideology and politics.[2]

De Lorean describes the process this way:

As I grew in General Motors it became apparent that objective criteria were not always used to evaluate an executive's performance. Many times the work record of a man who was promoted was far inferior to the records of others around him who were not promoted. It was quite obvious that something different than job performance was being used to rate these men.

That something different was a very subjective criterion which encompassed style, appearance, personality and, most importantly, personal loyalty to the man (or men) who was the promoter, and to the system which brought this all about. There were rules of this fraternity of management at GM. Those pledges willing to obey the rules were promoted. In the vernacular, they were the company's "team players." Those who didn't fit into the mold of a manager, who didn't adhere to the rules because they thought they were silly, generally weren't promoted. "He's not a team player," was the frequent, and many times only, objection to an executive in line for promotion. It didn't mean he was doing a poor job. It meant he didn't fit neatly into a stereotype of style, appearance and manner. He didn't display blind loyalty to the system of management, to the man or men doing the promoting. He rocked the boat. He took unpopular stands on products or policy which contradicted the prevailing attitude of top management. (40)

Keller (1989) adumbrates this point:

Elitism within the system was inevitable. Over the years it has become easy for executives to buy staff loyalty; everyone knows that's how you get on the fast-track—in GM lingo that's called being a HI-POT, a high-potential employee. At General Motors, the road to the corporate dining room is paved with occasions of looking the other way, of saying yes, of supporting the team, of keeping one's opinions to oneself. Those chosen few—about four thousand in number—who have achieved bonus-eligible status continue to be yes-sayers, their huge bonus earnings buying their loyalty. (33)

She notes this about current chairman Roger Smith:

For thirty-one years, Smith moved up through the ranks of GM as the consummate corporate player—the GM culture coursed in his veins. Admiration for and loyalty to the organization was at the core of his being. He was one of a new breed of corporate politicians whose success depended on their ease in wearing the corporate mantle. Translated, that meant, "Above all, be loyal to your superior's agenda." (66)

One result of this kind of collusion is that individuals who are retained and promoted are those who know very well how things are *supposed to look,* according to the ideology of the dominant coalition, but who know less and less about reality insofar as it conflicts with or simply is independent of this ideology. The problem is, of course, that since no organization is, or can be, the organization ideal, individuals who are retained and promoted are those who can cut themselves loose from discrepant reality.

Another result of this sort of selection must be that realistic and concerned persons must lose the belief that the organization's real purpose is productive work and come to the conclusion that its real purpose is self-promotion. They then are likely to see their work as being alien to the purposes of the organization and must find doing work increasingly depressing and useless.

De Lorean puts it this way:

In any system where inexperience and even incompetence exists in the upper reaches of management, lower-echelon executives become demoralized and dissatisfied. They see a system which impedes rather than enhances decision making. Their own jobs become frustrating. Divisional managers reporting to a group executive who is uneducated in their businesses must literally try to teach the business to him before getting decisions from him on their proposals. We often waltzed our bosses on the Fourteenth Floor through a step-by-step explanation of each program proposal—what it meant, how it related to the rest of the business and what it would do for the company. Even after this, their judgement most often was based on what GM had done before. (255)

And he gives this example of the clash between the incompetent who have been promoted and their competent but discouraged subordinates:

Increasingly, group and upper managers seemed to look upon their jobs in such narrow terms that it was impossible to competently direct broad corporate policy. Often misplaced, unprepared or simply undertalented, these executives filled their days and our committee meetings with minutiae. After one particularly frustrating meeting of the Administrative Committee, John Beltz and I were picking up our notes when he looked down at the far end of the conference table at the corporate management and said to me, "I wouldn't let one of those guys run a gas station for me." It was a bitter and sad indictment of our top management by one of the then young, truly bright lights of General Motors management. (256)

A third effect, obvious by this point, is that higher management is effectively isolated from criticism, or even serious discussion, of its thought and actions.[3]

De Lorean gives this account:

This system quickly shut top management off from the real world because it surrounded itself in many cases with "yes" men. There soon became no real vehicle for adequate outside input. Lower executives, eager to please the boss and rise up the corporate ladder, worked hard to learn what he wanted or how he thought on a particular subject. They then either fed the boss exactly what he wanted to know, or they modified their own proposals to suit his preferences.

Original ideas were often sacrificed in deference to what the boss wanted. Committee meetings no longer were forums for open discourse, but rather either soliloquies by the top man, or conversations between a few top men with the rest of the meeting looking on. In Fourteenth Floor meetings, often only three people, Cole, Gerstenberg, and Murphy would have anything substantial to say, even though there were 14 or 15 executives present. The rest of the team would remain silent, speaking only when spoken to. When they did offer a comment, in many cases it was just to paraphrase what had already been said by one of the top guys. (47)

Indeed, as organizational promotion and retention criteria shift toward the dramatization of the perfection of the organization, this shapes the very job of the subordinate into what Janis (1982) calls "mindguarding," the suppression of criticism.[4]

Keller also comments on the conflict between what one needs to do to get promoted and the quality of one's work:

> One retired executive rails against a system that creates vertical thinkers and cautious leaders. "The whole system stinks once you're in it. You continue to want to make vertical decisions: 'What is it that I should decide that will be good for me. Never make a horizontal decision based on what is good for the company. I want to get promoted.'
>
> So you get promoted because you're sponsored by someone; you get promoted before they catch up with you. I can go through a litany of those clowns. They go from this plant to that complex and then, all of a sudden, they've got plaques all over the walls that say how great they've done—but the plant's falling apart and the division's falling apart." (34)

The Creation of the Organizational Jungle

The more successful the organization is at projecting the image of itself as the organization ideal, the more deeply must committed participants experience anxiety. For the image projected, the image of the individual as perfectly a part of the perfect organization, is only an image; and the more perfect it is, the more acute the discrepancy between the *role* and the *role-player*. Given the importance of the organization ideal in the individual's self-concept, the individual must find some way to reconcile the discrepancy between the centrality in a loving world he or she is supposed to be experiencing and the wretchedness he or she in fact feels. As we have seen, the typical way is to attempt to deepen the identity of self and organization by rising in the organization's hierarchy and by fighting off what are perceived as threats to the organizational identity one has attained—perceived threats that are often projections of one's own self-doubts.

The result is that individuals become obsessed with organizational rank. They become compelled to beat down anyone whom they see as threatening or competing with them in their pursuit of higher rank or threatening the rank they have already acquired. Thus, ironically, behind the display of the organization ideal, of everyone working together to realize shared values, the real motivational process becomes a Hobbesian battle of one narcissism project against another narcissism project.[5] The consequences of this for coordination, cooperation, and motivation are clear enough. De Lorean says:

> Not only is the system perpetuating itself, but in the act of perpetuating itself the system has fostered several destructive practices which are harmful to executive morale. They developed from the psychological need, as I see it, of less competent managers to affirm in their own minds a logical right to their positions, even though the basis for their promotions was illogical by any business-performance standard. Once in a position of power, a manager who was promoted by the system is insecure because, consciously or not, he knows that it was something other than his ability to manage and his knowledge of the business that put him in his position. . . . He thus looks for methods and defense mechanisms to ward off threats to his power. (49)

Isolation of Management and Rupture of Communications

A related problem is that the greater the success of the totalitarian manager, the more the manager is isolated from his or her subordinates. The world the subordinates live in is the world of the organization ideal as created by the totalitarian manager. The world that the totalitarian manager lives in is the world of the *construction of the image* of the organization ideal. These two worlds are incommensurable, and communication and trust cannot help but break down between them. For communication and trust mean two different things to these groups. Indeed, for totalitarian management, communication to subordinates is not communication at all—it is deception.[6]

The practice of totalitarian management indicates contempt on the part of the manager toward the managed. Such managers do not believe that the managed have the capacity, for whatever reason, to come to the correct view on the basis of the simple presentation of facts. Thus, the fact that the presentation is a presentation and the contempt that it implies must be covered-up. And then the cover-up must be covered up, and so on, in the manner that Argyris (1985) has described.

In this fashion, the organization comes to be stratified in an insider/outsider dimension, which in chapter 2 I likened to the structure of an onion and which serves the same function as party membership in the totalitarian state. This must make a mockery of all attempts to break down status barriers that stand in the way of effective communication—as appears to be the idea behind various "quality of working life" efforts.

Development of Hostile Orientation Toward the Environment

If the totalitarian manager is successful, organizational participants take the organization as an organization ideal. It must follow, in their thinking, that such an organization will be successful in its dealings with the world. As we saw in chapter 3, this poses a difficulty of interpretation for the necessarily problematic relationships between the organization and its environment.

Thus, as we know, the environment places constant demands on the organization. Failure to meet them will result in the organization's death. But from the standpoint of the totalitarian manager committed to portraying the organization as the organization ideal, this sort of reasoning cannot be acknowledged. From this point of view it is the organization that is the criterion of worth. The environment is not conceived to exist as an independent environment at all; it exists only in order to support the organization. From this standpoint the demands of the environment must be presented as hostile actions by bad external forces—hostile actions to which a legitimate response is equally hostile action.

The General Motors Corporation, in response to Ralph's Nader's book about the Corvair, *Unsafe at Any Speed* (1965), hired private detectives to find ways to discredit him. As De Lorean remarks, "When Nader's book threatened the Corvair's sales and profits, he became an enemy of the system. Instead of trying to attack his credentials or the factual basis of his arguments, the company sought to attack him personally" (64).

Sending private detectives to find out the details of his private life suggests something about the company managers' attitude toward him. It suggests that they expected to find something to show that he was a bad person. He had to be a bad person: he had attacked GM, hadn't he? Thus, notes De Lorean, "Criticism from the outside is generally viewed as ill-informed. General Motors management thinks what it is doing is right, because it is GM that is doing it and the outside world is wrong. It is always 'they' versus 'us'." (257).

Another incident De Lorean describes confirms the point:

> When a reputable Harvard management professor, Peter Drucker, in 1946 wrote *The Concept of a Corporation,* which dissected and analyzed General Motors, the public regarded the work as decidedly pro-business and pro-GM.

But the corporation didn't. . . . He was resoundingly criticized within the company for daring to criticize the organization of the corporation. (258)

Thus, the picture of the organization as organization ideal leads to an orientation toward the world that can best be described as paranoid. It is clear enough that such a conception must degrade the relationships with the environment that the organization requires for its survival.

The Transposition of Work and Ritual

When work, the productive process, becomes display, its meaning becomes lost. Its performance as part of the organizational drama becomes the only meaning it has. Accordingly, the parts it plays in the organization's transactions with the world become irrelevant. When this happens, work loses its adaptive function and becomes mere ritual.

At the same time, the rituals that serve to express the individual's identification with the organization ideal, especially those connected with rank, come to be infused with significance for the individual. They become sacred. Thus, reality and appearance trade places. The energy that once went into the production of goods and services of value to others is channeled into the dramatization of a narcissistic fantasy in which the organization's environment is merely a stage setting.

Consider how this shows up in the matter of dress. One can easily make a case that patterns of dress among organizational participants often have some functionality. But when the issue comes to be invested with great meaning, one must suspect that ritual has supplanted function. De Lorean gives some examples:

At General Motors, good appearance meant conservative dress. In my first meeting as a GM employee in 1956 at Pontiac, half the session was taken up in discussion about some vice-president downtown at headquarters who was sent home that morning for wearing a brown suit. Only blue or black suits were tolerated then. I remember thinking that was silly. But in those days I followed the rules closely. (40–41)

Later on, when he was less inclined to follow the rules just because they were the rules, De Lorean found out what violation of them meant:

I made a habit of widening my circle of friends and broadening my tastes. This awareness precipitated a seemingly endless chain of personality conflicts, the most difficult of which was with Roger Keyes, who was my boss while I was running Pontiac and Chevrolet divisions. He made life unbearable for me, and he was dedicated to getting me fired; he told me so, many times. Fortunately, I had the protection of my ability as I ran those two divisions to fend off Keyes. But I remember vividly my conflicts with him, especially when he was irritated by my style of dress. The corporate rule was dark suits, light shirts and muted ties. I followed the rule to the letter, only I wore stylish Italian-cuts suits, wide collared off-white shirts and wide ties.

"Goddamit, John," he'd yell. "Can't you dress like a businessman? And get your hair cut, too."

My hair was ear length with sideburns. (9–10)

The dynamics of the ways in which ritual comes to assume the importance work should have help to explain the dynamics of the ritualization of work. For the willingness to allow one's behavior to be determined by meaningless rituals comes to be justified by an idealization of the organization that elevates its customs above and discredits one's values—one's sense of what is important. This willingness to subordinate and delegitimate—in a word to repress—one's own sense of what is important, even about matters that should be within the competence of anyone's judgment, must have its consequences magnified when the matters in question become more abstruse and difficult to make judgments about, as is the case with real executive work. Then the repression of one's values deprives one of any basis for making such judgments and leads naturally to a superimposition of the rituals with which one is familiar, even where, patently, they do not belong. This is what gives the horror to De Lorean's story about what he found when he was elevated to the Fourteenth Floor, GM's executive suite, as group executive in charge of the domestic Car and Truck Group:

When I finally moved upstairs . . . I saw that the job . . . often consisted only of . . . little, stupid, make-work kinds of assignments, things which I thought should have been decided further down the line.

Some of these things, which had little or no impact on the business, were an insult to a person's intelligence. . . . As I recall, [for example, my boss] asked me to catalogue service parts numbers and to prepare reports on the size of parts inventories. . . .

"This is supposed to be a planning job," I remember thinking. "But I feel like a file clerk. I've spent many years learning to be a good executive. Now I can't use that knowledge."

. . . I set up a meeting with Vice-Chairman Tom Murphy, to whom I had reported when he held the job I now held. . . .

"Tom, I think I know what has to be done for the long-term health of GM But I don't get any time to work on it. I just don't get any time to plan my days because of this array of meetings, inane assignments and tons of endless paperwork."

He responded, "Hell, John, when I had that job I never got to plan one minute. It was completely planned for me. The job just drags you from place to place. You don't have time to plan. It is not that kind of job.". . .

"Well that's exactly what's happening to me, and I don't consider it satisfactory," I said. "The system is deciding what I should be working on and what is important; I'm not. I'm not doing any planning of the direction of the company, and this is a planning job. No one else seems to be planning either. We're in for trouble . . ." . . .

Murphy didn't say much further. I suddenly realized that what I felt was a weakness of life on the Fourteenth Floor, he and others thought was "business as usual." They were quite happy to let their jobs drag them from one place to the next, trying to solve problems as they came up, but not getting into the kind of long-range planning that Fourteenth Floor executives were supposed to be doing.[7] . . . I later mentioned my frustration to [President Ed] Cole and he told me: "You've got to go through the steps. This job is part of the process." That process didn't seem very attractive and fulfilling to me.

So I quit doing the things I thought weren't worthwhile to the job. . . .

It quickly evolved that I wasn't a "member of the team." (26–34)

De Lorean explains the matter of management ritual, as opposed to work, this way:

A promotional system which stressed "loyalty to the boss" more than performance put into top management executives who, while hard-working, nevertheless lacked the experience, and in some cases the ability to manage capably or guide the business. The preoccupation on the Fourteenth Floor with the appearance of working—putting in long hours, going through the motions of the job, occupying time with minutiae—is a direct result of management's inability to grasp the scope of its job and grapple with the problems that arise. (250)

Loss of Creativity

The delegitimation of one's sense of what is important gives rise to a special case of the ritualization of work—the loss of creativity. Schein (1983) describes the condition of "conformity" that follows from an insistence by the organization that all of its norms be accepted as being equally important. Under that condition, the individual "can tune in so completely on what he sees to be the way others are handling themselves that he becomes a carbon-copy and sometimes a caricature of them."

Consequently, Schein notes: "The conforming individual curbs his creativity and thereby moves the organization toward a sterile form of bureaucracy" (1980).

Maslow (1970) gives insight into the psychodynamics of this process when he observes that creativity is characteristic of both ends of the continuum of personality development, but not of the stages in the middle (170–71). Creativity, this suggests, is a function of spontaneity, a function of taking seriously our actual affects and interacting in the world in consideration of our spontaneous feelings. But as the self comes to be dominated by a concern for how things appear to others, which is characteristic of the middle stages of personality development (Schwartz 1983b), creativity disappears as a mode of interacting with the world. As the organization requires that the individual subordinate his or her spontaneous perception to an uncritical acceptance of the ideal character of the organization, it thus determines that the affective basis of creativity will be repressed.

The lack of creativity, since it is a lack of something, cannot be positively demonstrated. As an experience, it makes itself known as a feeling of missing something different that has not occurred, even though one does not know what the different element would have been. Thus, De Lorean found himself introducing a "new" crop of Chevrolets that were not really new at all:

This whole show is nothing but a replay of last year's show, and the year before that and the year before that. The speech I just gave was the same speech I gave last year, written by the same guy in public relations about the same superficial product improvements as previous years. . . . Almost nothing has changed. . . . there was nothing new and revolutionary in car development and there hadn't been for years. (60–61)

In benign times, one may experience boredom: the consciousness of a sameness, a lack of originality. When circumstances are harsh, partly as a result of the lack of creativity that the organization needed if it was to have adapted, one may simply experience the intractability of the situation. Adding up the figures in the usual way simply shows one, again and again, how hopeless the situation is. One may then experience the loss of creativity as a wish for a savior who will make the organization's problems disappear.

In the hard times, I suspect, one rarely comes to recognize that the ideas that the organization needed in order to have avoided its present hopeless state may have been upon the scene a long time ago. But the individuals who had them might have been passed over for promotion because they were not "team players," or perhaps they were made to feel uncomfortable because they did not fit it in, or maybe they were scapegoated whenever the organization needed a victim. Indeed, ironically, the very ideas that were needed might have been laughed at or ignored because they were not "the way we do things around here."

Dominance of the Financial Staff

Another hypothesis may be used to account for the emergent dominance of the financial function of the corporation that De Lorean found in General Motors and that others, for example Halberstam (1986) have partly blamed for the decline of American industry.

As envisioned by Alfred P. Sloan, the financial function and the operations side of the corporation were both supposed to be represented strongly at the top level of the corporation. But, as De Lorean notes, over time, and specifically through the rise of Frederick Donner, the financial side came to dominate the corporation. Why?

I propose that finance, rather than operations, offers the greater narcissistic possibilities. As Nader and Taylor (1986) note, operations, the productive process, tends to temper grandiosity. The recalcitrance of matter, so to speak, exerts a humbling influence. Not so with finance. I suggest that the financial worldview can be understood as a kind of latter-day Pythagoreanism in which the world is seen as mere instantiation of number, and as imposing no bounds on the imagination's flights. Everything seems possible as long as the numbers can be made to work, and the one who can make them work can take this as a sign of omnipotence. When the matter comes to competitive elevation of the organization ideal, who can do it better, who can represent it better than the officer whose bonds to earthly substance are the lightest. Who better than the specialist in finance?

Keller's analysis is similar:

Financial people operate in a rarefied environment. For them, solving a problem means successfully juggling the numbers on financial statements. What happens when the numbers determine every major investment and product initiative? Reality gets distorted. (26–27)

Then she goes on to say:

The tyranny of the numbers crunchers has evolved, to a great extent, from GM's reluctance to hear bad news about itself. If the finance guys can present the right numbers, everyone breathes a sigh of relief, and the finance people look like heroes. There's no incentive for executives in finance positions to give bad news; the more facile they can be with numbers, the higher their fortunes rise. (27–28)

Cynicism and Corruption; or, Self-Deception and the Narcissistic Loss of Reality

Referring to the ways people are related to their own presentations, Goffman (1959:17–18) notes that one can either be taken in by one's own performance or not taken in by it. In the latter case, the individual uses it only "to guide the conviction of his audience . . . as a means to other ends." Such an individual is a cynic, disassociating him- or herself from discrepant information consciously and through deception. In the former case, the individual "comes to be performer and observer of the same show." Goffman adds:

It will have been necessary for the individual in his performing capacity to conceal from himself in his audience capacity the discreditable facts that he has had to learn about the performance; in everyday terms, there will be things he knows, or has known, that he will not be able to tell himself. (81)

Goffman notes that these persons cut themselves loose from discrepant information through repression and disassociation, a point that corresponds perfectly with psychoanalytic theory concerning the maintenance of the ego ideal. Such individuals are self-deceptive. Thus, in the totalitarian organization, no matter what its espoused values, promotion and even continued inclusion will tend to go to deceptive cynics, whose moral involvement in their organizational activity is attenuated, or to self-deceptive persons, whose involvement in reality is attenuated.

Of the two, it is difficult to say which is to be preferred. Cynics at least know what is going on around them; and if their moral involvement in their organizational role is attenuated, that does not seem inappropriate in an organization managed by deceptive and totalitarian means. Indeed, in organizations that have seriously degenerated as a result of these processes, it is often only the cynics who can get anything done at all.

Nonetheless, there is no doubt that cynicism tends toward corruption. Corruption does not play a major role in De Lorean's picture of General Motors, but he does note its presence: "there were disturbing activities in upper management in which executives used their positions of power and knowledge to profit *personally* in corporate business" (83). My analysis leads me to suspect that, as time goes by, if GM continues to deteriorate, it will become increasingly difficult for even minimally functioning individuals to idealize it. Then, corruption will increasingly become a problem.

For the present, I think the more serious problem comes in with those who deceive themselves and distance themselves from reality. For as the processes I have described operate and as the organization degenerates accordingly, it becomes increasingly difficult to see it as the ideal, and individuals who are able to do so must become increasingly self-deceptive. A point must come when such individuals may not be said to be psychologically living in the same world that the real organization is in. Worse, since this capacity for self-deception is an important advantage in the race for promotion, the total disassociation of the individual from organizational reality is likely to be correlated with the individual's position in the hierarchy. Then the most important processes within the organization come to be under the authority of people who are not operating in the real world as far as the organization's requirements are concerned.

Keller hints at this in a way that will be of increased importance in the conclusion.

During the 1970's, a writer for *Fortune* magazine set out on a quest for dissenting views at General Motors, and found it hard "to find a top executive at GM who does not evidence enthusiasm for what he or the company is doing." One view might hold that GM had achieved a state of management consensus that would be the envy of any company. But more likely, the lack of dissension was motivated by self-interest. It was managerial suicide to be the person who got labeled a naysayer. *There was also an element of denial; in the same way that children of alcoholics often refuse to accept their parents' addiction, GM employees refused to admit the truth about their corporate parent. They didn't want to believe.* (65–66, emphasis added)

Overcentralization

The narcissistic loss of reality among those at the top of the corporation may be a major cause of overcentralization of operational decision-making. De Lorean found this overcentralization in General Motors, and with it the tendency to provide simplistic answers to complex questions. The idea that, having risen to the top of the corporation, individuals would hold themselves as bearing all of its knowledge and virtues follows immediately from what I have been saying.

Thus, top management would be likely to believe themselves more capable than anyone else of providing answers to any questions that arise. Having no command of specific details beyond those in their imaginations, the answers that they give, and that would come to bind the rest of the corporation, would necessarily be simplistic and inappropriate. Moreover, as the decay process continues, and as the competence of top management declines accordingly, both their tendency to impose simple answers to complex problems and the specific inadequacy even of the simplistic answers they propose would tend to increase. Moreover, the capacity of the system to correct itself would tend to decrease, since the increasing power of the higher echelons of the corporation, and their increasing narcissism, would tend toward an attribution of blame to the lower levels of the organization. This would delegitimate those whose judgment would be necessary to reverse the decay process.

De Lorean provides a number of examples. Here is one:

The corporate program for maximum standardization of parts across product lines was a knee-jerk cost-cutting reaction to the incredible proliferation of models, engines and parts which took place in the uncontrolled and unplanned boom of the 1960's. However, the program was not intelligently thought out. It was not thoroughly analyzed for its actual effect on the company. On paper the concept looked good and seemed like a sure way to save money. In reality it wasted money. The car divisions rebelled at various stages of the standardization program. Their cries were unanswered. When Chevrolet rebelled against using the new corporate U-joint . . . Keyes told me, "Use the corporate one or I'll get someone in Chevy who will."

We used it, at an investment of about $16 million in tooling, and our costs rose $1.40 per car. In addition, the corporate design failed in use and Chevy paid out about $5 million extra in warranty claims.

Instead of saving money, the standardization program at GM wound up costing the corporation about $300 million extra per year. . . .

The last straw came in 1972, however, when management asked us: "Why is the cost of building a Chevrolet $70 closer to Oldsmobile today than it was in 1964?" The question from the top was offered in the usual "you aren't doing your job" manner. The irony was incredible. (252–53)

Keller's observations of this sort of overcentralization offer a true embarrassment of riches, especially with regard to the attempt to impose simplistic answers to complex problems. Indeed, her account is in some ways even more devastating because of its broader scope and because of the higher price-tag that came, in time, to be attached to errors of this type. Perhaps the most important case she reports concerns the tremendous capital investment GM made in high technology factories during the 1980s. Her overall verdict:

GM's high-tech plants were failures that have triggered a technology backlash in the company. It is estimated that as much as 20 percent of the capital investments made in plant modernization has been wasted and substantial amounts of machinery have been scrapped. GM ends the decade with its plants unable to build cars as productively as Ford, which has yet to modernize most of its facilities. Furthermore, the investment program was based on the assumption that GM's market share would blossom, necessitating the use of all facilities at full capacity. With a shrinking share, it was pointless to spend some of the billions on new assembly plants and stamping plants since the decreased penetration didn't warrant it. (254)

And the cause of all this waste:

GM's massive capital-spending programs substituted fixed costs for variable costs and were undertaken in a profoundly mistaken belief that the main reason for high production costs in the past were strictly a function of excessive compensation to hourly workers and overmanning of the assembly line.

To which she adds:

Ironically, even as they invested fortunes in solving the productivity problem, their man-hours per car remained higher than both Chrysler and Ford. (213)

The Magical Flight to Utopia

Another manifestation of the narcissistic loss of reality is the tendency of the decadent organization, recognizing its beleaguerment, to take recourse in a fantasy of saving itself through an act that will be qualitatively different from anything it has done before. Typically, the act will involve some new concept, the invocation of which will have the magical power of transforming the organization directly into the organization ideal.[8]

For General Motors, this sort of utopian thinking appeared full-blown in the 1980s with the accession of Roger Smith to the chairmanship. Keller, again, gives a number of examples of this, and GM's orgy of spending on high technology may certainly be seen in this light. Perhaps the clearest example was the Saturn project.

Launched in 1983 with a $5 billion investment, the Saturn project was supposed to build a car that would be competitive with Japanese imports. But GM never conceived of it as just a new car. It was to be a whole new approach to the auto business in totality. It would be developed at Saturn and then used to transform all of GM.

Keller quotes recommendations from the final report of the Advance Product Manufacturing and Engineering staff, which recommended the project. Its goals were:

1. The establishment of a car-building project that was not just a vehicle program, but an integrated business process.
2. To operate the project as a wholly owned subsidiary of GM, with a separate union-management relationship.
3. The creation of a separate dealership franchise to operate in conjunction with the project.
4. The development of a new car for the 1990's that would be completely unique in design and structure.

What seems clear enough is the element of fantasy that runs through the Saturn program. As NASA did with the space shuttle (see chapter 7), GM seemed to be invoking a deity that could rescue the company from its own past and present.

But GM could never create a god. All it could do, at its best, was build a car. Indulging in this sort of fantasy would, paradoxically, make the company in many ways *less* able to build good cars since GM would have to discard what it knew about making cars that had retained its validity along with what had lost it. Thus, Keller quotes a letter from Glenn T. Wilson, an associate professor of operations management, to the *Wall Street Journal:*

GM's Saturn project aims at producing a new car at a new location with new methods and new workers. It might work, but it will require superhuman efforts to avoid producing a bumper crop of lemons.

What would be preferable? If you want to build a new "green field" auto factory (a dubious idea anyway, when there's so much surplus capacity), it should produce a standard model of car. If you want to test high-tech robots, do it at an existing factory where the workers already know what they're doing. If you want to produce a small cheap car, do it at an existing plant where the machinery is already fully depreciated. And if you want a cheap car design, why not produce a two-seater designed for local travel by normal-size people, instead of a sedan for a family of four midgets. (224)

Taken all together, then, it is not difficult to see how the result would be that, as Lee Iacocca put it in his book *Talking Straight* (cited by Keller, 223): "Sure enough, little by little, Saturn is coming unglued."[9]

AN OVERVIEW

Before concluding this discussion of the practical consequences of totalitarian management, it is worthwhile to note a characteristic that the consequences mentioned have in common: they are all cumulative and interactive with each other. They all tend to build within the system and, interacting with each other, take over the system bit by bit. This is the way in which the ineffectiveness characteristic of the decadent organization becomes systemic and generalized. Thus, for example, the accumulation of bad decisions taken within the system suggests that those who manifest belief in it as an organization ideal must increasingly be self-deceptive or cynical, which in turn decreases the retention of realism and concern for work, which leads to a further increase in bad decisions, further degradation of the relationship with the environment, and so on.

The result of this is that the *rate* of decay will tend to accelerate. That GM's market share took six years to decline from 46 percent to 41 percent, but only three more years to go to 35 percent now comes to make a certain chilling sense.

One more observation is worth making in this connection. It is that, beyond a certain point, the decay process becomes essentially irreversible. It no longer makes sense, after this point, to say that the organization needs to do "this" or "that" in order to bring the organization back to health. The problem is that there is no such thing as "the organization" that can make such changes apart from its management. But its management has been successfully selected for its incapacity, as far as dealing in reality is concerned. They cannot solve the problem of the organization. They *are* the problem. I fear that General Motors may be in this condition.

CONCLUSION: ON AVERTING ORGANIZATIONAL DECAY

There is no doubt that fantasy plays an important part in our mental lives. To say this one does not need either to approve of fantasy or to regret its inroads into the psyche. Fantasy simply *is*. So it is with the ego ideal, which is a particularly central fantasy in our lives.

But the same cannot be said for organizational totalitarianism and organizational decay. These are neither necessary nor inevitable features of organizational life. They become features of organizational life when the *desire* to be the center of a loving world becomes a *demand* and when the *power* is available to turn this demand into a program of action.

What this suggests is that organizational totalitarianism and organizational decay, which might appear to be systemic problems that concern the organization, are at their root existential, moral, even spiritual, problems that concern the individual, and that these problems at the individual level become systemic problems for the organization when organizational power is used to effect this transformation.

Putting the matter this way suggests a connection between this analysis of organizational decay, on the one hand, and the Greek conception of tragedy, on the other. What is evident in both cases is the horror that comes from the claims of powerful mortals to be more than mortal. The Greeks called this *hubris* and they knew that the gods, whom we might refer to as reality, do not stand for it. They demand humility.

5

Organizational Disaster and Organizational Decay: The Case of the National Aeronautics and Space Administration

Explanations of disasters often assume that the disaster was the result of a single, isolated decision that was wrongly made. Indeed, it is typically asserted that the decision-making process employed was one that is ordinarily valid but that, in the specific case, crossed over some vague boundary and led to the disaster.

Explanations like this take for granted that the organizational context of the decision was basically sound. Set against the presumed backdrop of the organization's continuing healthy activity, the decision and the disaster that followed from it are seen as an aberration, an unfortunate accident—as much a tragedy for the well-meaning and generally competent individuals who made the decision as for its more direct victims.

While this scenario is certainly accurate in many instances, there are other cases in which an opposing vision may be closer to the facts. Here, the specific decision is seen as fundamentally flawed and as taking place within a generally unsound organizational context. Indeed, from this point of view, the decision is only one of many bad decisions that the unhealthy organization generates naturally and almost inexorably.

But traditional organization theory does not enable us to understand organizations that are fundamentally unhealthy. Our theories of organization are basically functionalist theories, which assume that organizational processes make sense in terms of the overall purposes of the organization. Within this paradigm, these overall purposes go unquestioned, and the validity of the fundamental organizational processes that carry them through is taken for granted. Thus, within this paradigm, organizational disasters and the bad decisions that lead up to them *must* be seen as aberrations.

The purpose of this chapter and the next is to show how the theory of organizational decay can be used for the analysis of organizational disaster. Through the process of decay, an organization can become basically unsound; rational process can become the aberration, rather than faulty decision-making and disaster. In this chapter, I will illustrate this process of decay by an analysis of the history of the United States National Aeronautics and Space Administration as it led up to the *Challenger* disaster. In the next chapter, I will analyze the *Challenger* disaster on the basis of the theory of the organization ideal, a theory that comes more and more to describe an organization as it decays.

THE *CHALLENGER* DISASTER AS AN ABERRATION

It will be useful to begin the analysis by considering more traditional orientations to the *Challenger* disaster. In an article on organizational culture and reliability, Weick (1988) reasoned:

> When people think they have a problem solved, they often let up, which means they stop making continuous adjustments. When the shuttle flights continued to depart and return successfully, the criterion for a launch—convince me that I should send the Challenger—was dropped. Underestimating the dynamic nature of reliability, managers inserted a new criterion—convince me that I shouldn't send Challenger. (25)

Similarly, Starbuck and Milliken (1988) maintained that the catastrophe was the result of "fine-tuning" that had gone too far. For them, the disaster arose in the context of a natural intra-organizational conflict between managers and engineers:

> Engineers are taught to place very high priority on quality and safety. If engineers are not sure whether a product is safe enough, they are supposed to make it much safer than they believe necessary. . . .
> [But] safety factors are, by definition, supposed to be unnecessary. . . . To reduce waste and to make good use of capacity, an organization needs to cut safety factors down. . . .
> . . . successful experiences make safety factors look more and more wasteful. . . .
> Although engineers may propose cost savings, their emphasis on quality and safety relegates cost to a subordinate priority. Managers, on the other hand, are expected to pursue cost reduction and capacity utilization, so it is managers who usually propose cuts in safety factors. (333)

Thus, incremental reduction in safety factors on the basis of successful experience, a form of what Starbuck and Milliken call "fine-tuning," is a normal and natural organizational process—a part, indeed of the manager's job. And it is natural, normal, and even commonplace to pursue it until disaster happens. The point is not to stop the fine-tuning, but to learn from the disasters that it inevitably creates on the road to progress.

In these arguments, there is no hint that there was anything wrong with NASA. Indeed, Weick is even worried that a loss of faith in NASA's reliability will have the effect of *decreasing* its reliability. For reliability is "dynamic" and grows out of faith in the reliability of the system. This faith makes it possible for the system to act. Then, vigilance in the course of the action creates the reliability that had been assumed. Thus:

> The importance of faith in holding a system together in ways that reduce errors has been discussed for some time as "The Right Stuff." . . .
> While this mechanism is sometimes interpreted as macho bravado, it is important to remember that confidence is just as important in the production of reliability as is doubt. The mutually exclusive character of these two determinants can be seen in the growing doubt among astronauts that they have been flying the safe system they thought they were. Notice that the system itself has not suddenly changed character. (27–28)

But a closer look at the context of the *Challenger* disaster reveals difficulties with these analyses. First of all, the decision to launch the *Challenger* was not based on a sound principle that was overapplied. Second, NASA was far from being healthy. Let us take these one at a time.

To begin with, Starbuck and Milliken's claim that managers were trying to remove unnecessary safety factors is incorrect because there were no safety factors, and the managers were blind not to know this. The fact is that the shuttle flights were not successes. Many of them were near-catastrophes and had been so for a long time. Below I note a number of system components that regularly had serious problems. Here I shall mention only a few that related specifically to the SRB O-rings:

1. As early as October 1977, NASA rejected as "unacceptable" Morton-Thiokol's design for solid rocket booster (SRB) seals because "joint rotation" prevented the secondary O-rings from sealing.

2. After tests performed in May 1982, NASA "Accepted the conclusion that the secondary O-ring was no longer functional . . . when the Solid Rocket Motor reached 40 percent of its maximum expected oper-

ating pressure" (Rogers Commission [RC] 1986: 126) and therefore ruled the seal system nonredundant.

3. In-flight erosion of the primary seal occurred as early as the second shuttle flight, in November 1981, and, beginning with flight 41-B in February 1984, it became a regular occurrence, with some primary O-rings not sealing at all.

4. On flight 51-B, not only did a primary O-ring fail altogether to seal, but a secondary O-ring eroded.

Thus, NASA knew that it could depend on neither the secondary O-ring nor the primary O-ring. It also knew, of course, that if neither O-ring sealed, the result would be catastrophic. This condition was deemed so serious that NASA issued a launch constraint on all subsequent flights —and then waived it in each case.[1]

The second premise, that the system was healthy, also turns out to be false. Rather, a closer look at the organizational context shows that, despite Weick's claim, there certainly *was* something wrong at NASA. Indeed, the system *had* changed its character. To be sure, it had not changed suddenly. Nonetheless, over the years, NASA had become a hollow shell of its former self.

Consider the problems that had arisen in four cross-cutting dimensions:

1. Hardware Problems: The solid rocket booster joints that were found to have caused the *Challenger* explosion were far from being the only unreliable items in the shuttle system. On the contrary, the Rogers Commission found that the wheel, braking, and steering systems were all faulty and that the main engines had a number of serious problems, including cracks in the turbine blades, valve failures and leaks from heat exchangers.

2. Loss of Administrative Control: NASA had virtually lost control of its spending and had wasted, according to federal audits, at least $3.5 billion:

In the last 15 years, . . . bad administration and spending abuses have been found in virtually every aspect of the NASA operations, from running the shuttle to developing planetary probes, from satellites to construction of buildings, from space experiments to employee overtime, from headquarters to field centers, according to the [General Accounting Office] documents. (*New York Times*, 23 April 1986)

3. Loss of Technical Control: In its early years, NASA had maintained the technological capability and the staff to oversee its contractors. Indeed,

[James Webb, NASA Administrator from 1961 to 1968] would not allow NASA to fall behind its contractors technically. He demanded that NASA employees always know more about their programs than the contractors working for them. When the electronics of Apollo seemed to go beyond the agency's knowledge, Webb pushed through a NASA electronics center at MIT. (Trento 1987: 56)

By 1982 this technological capability had been lost, and contractors had become free to do whatever they wanted with impunity (Trento 1987: 208–9, 239; *New York Times*, 29 June 1986, Business section).

4. Loss of Control over Operations: NASA came to have extreme and increasing difficulty in conducting and coordinating the complex processes involved in shuttle operations. The Rogers Commission, in assessing NASA's difficulties in this area, maintained that "an assessment of the system's overall performance is best made by studying the process at the end of the production chain: crew training" (166). And, in this regard, the commission quoted astronaut Henry Hartsfield:

"Had we not had the accident, we were going to be up against a wall; STS 61-H . . . would have had to average 31 hours in the simulator to accomplish their required training, and STS 61-K would have to average 33 hours [note normal time was 77 hours]. That is ridiculous. For the first time, somebody was going to have to stand up and say we have got to slip the launch because we are not going to have the crew trained." (170)

On the whole, the picture of NASA that emerges from thorough investigation is of an organization characterized by the generalized and systemic ineffectiveness that we associate with organizational decay— an organization in which the flawed decision to launch the *Challenger* was not an aberration but a normal and ordinary way of doing business. James Webb—the man who, more than any other single person, had built NASA—put it this way: "There was an organization that was regarded as being perfect, that suddenly doesn't do the simplest thing" (Trento 1987: vii).

Under the circumstances, the focus of inquiry into the *Challenger* disaster changes. The question becomes not how could a specific decision be made at a specific time, but instead concerns the organization as a whole. Specifically, the question concerns how an organization that "was regarded as being perfect," that placed men on the moon, could become an organization that "doesn't do the simplest thing."

SOME ASPECTS OF THE DECAY PROCESS

A number of aspects of organizational decay can be illustrated by the case of NASA. Some of them were discussed in the previous chapter. In this chapter, I shall organize these aspects into a three-part scheme. The first part is what I call the institutionalization of the fiction, which involves the redirection of its approved beliefs and discourse from the acknowledgement of reality to the maintenance of an image of itself as the organization ideal. Second is the change in personnel that parallels the institutionalization of the fiction. Third is the narcissistic loss of reality, which is the mental state of management in the decadent organization.

The Institutionalization of the Fiction

The Commitment to a Bad Decision. If the organization were the organization ideal, it would never make a bad decision. Since no organization is or can be the organization ideal, this means that they all make bad decisions sooner or later. The institutionalization of the fiction of the organization ideal begins when the organization, trying to justify its bad decision, becomes committed to it (see Staw 1980).

In the case of NASA, the original bad decision was to build the shuttle on the cheap. This decision was bad because the low figure for development that NASA accepted seriously compromised quality, and ruled out the original idea of a reusable shuttle system that could inexpensively and reliably carry payloads into orbit.

Denial of Reality Through the Idealization of the Organization. The underfunding that began at this point need not have caused the whole system to decay. What ensured it was that, having made a deal to develop the shuttle cheaply, members of NASA management magnified their sense of competence and believed that, since they were NASA, they could still realize the original idea of the space shuttle.

NASA had two strategies that could have led to a viable shuttle program. The original plan, which would certainly have been the best in the long run, was to build an adequately funded shuttle system that would have permitted cheap operation. The second feasible alternative was to build the shuttle cheaply and sharply restrict operations. The Nixon administration canceled the first possibility, but the second remained. However, the second strategy would have required NASA to recognize the severe limitations that the restricted developmental budget had placed on the shuttle, and it was this sense of limitation that they could not accept. Hence, they chose a third strategy: building the shuttle cheaply and maintaining its schedule. This strategy involved the denial of the reality of the shuttle system's limitations, countering it with a fantasy of the shuttle's perfection as a product of perfect NASA.

Senator and former astronaut John Glenn, interviewed on the news program *This Week with David Brinkley* (8 June 1986), described NASA's transition this way:

Well, I think there has been, and I think back in the days when I was in the program I think there was a can-do attitude, a go-for-it attitude, and safety was paramount. Bob Gilruth, when we first got in the program, told us back in those days, "You know, any time you have a question about safety, let me know and we'll stop, we'll change, we'll do additional tests, we'll do whatever." And I think that can-do attitude, perhaps at least with some people at NASA . . . was replaced by a can't-fail attitude, and I think that's unfortunate that that crept into the program.

And Eugene Cernan, another former astronaut, said on the same program: "I think they were just caught up with the fact that, 'Hey, we're infallible. We can't help but succeed.' "

Actually, there is evidence of totalitarianism, as described above, developing at NASA over the issue of maintaining the idea of building the shuttle cheaply.

Trento (1987) quotes NASA veteran John Naugle to this effect:

"I think Fletcher [NASA administrator under Nixon] felt sincerely that if he couldn't justify the shuttle economically, he couldn't make it go. And that was where my feeling was that if he had gone back to Nixon and said, 'There is no way Jose that I can justify this economically; we either do it as an R&D program because it ought to be done, or we go out of the manned space flight business.' " (119)

But Fletcher did not do that. Rather, when reality intruded upon NASA's idealization of itself, it appears that NASA suppressed reality. Thus, Naugle says:

"Up until that era there, I never worried about saying what I felt. I always felt my bosses . . . while they might not agree with me, they might slap me down, they might quarrel with me, but they were not going to throw me out just because I brought them bad news. And somewhere between the time Fletcher came on board and the time he left, I no longer felt that way." (121)

Further Decision-Making on the Basis of the Idealization of the Organization. Belief in the organization ideal determines actions. The fate of the *Challenger* was sealed by the decisions made on the basis of NASA's self-idealization.

A good example of the systemic nature of organizational decay was the decision to declare the shuttle "operational" after only four flights.

The Rogers Commission observed that the use of the term *operational* "has encountered some criticism because it erroneously suggests that the Shuttle had attained an airline-like degree of routine operation" (5). This connotation of the term *operational* is one that NASA bought into entirely, and as a result, NASA placed demands on the shuttle system that simply could not be met and that would have, according to many experts, resulted in disaster even if flight 51-L had been postponed. (For example, see Murray 1986.)

The Rogers Commission documents numerous problems that arose from the declaration of the shuttle as operational. One example, which will serve for all, is this:

The capabilities of the Shuttle processing and facilities support work force became increasingly strained as the Orbiter turnaround time decreased to accommodate the accelerated launch schedule. This factor has resulted in overtime percentages of almost 28 percent in some directorates. Numerous contract employees have worked 72 hours per week or longer and frequent 12-hour shifts. The potential implications of such overtime for safety were made apparent during the attempted launch of mission 61-C on January 6, 1986, when fatigue and shiftwork were cited as major contributing factors to a serious incident involving a liquid oxygen depletion that occurred less than five minutes before scheduled lift-off. (171)

From the point of view of the theory of the organization ideal, the concept that the shuttle was operational was a specification and extension of the organization ideal and had the effect of ramifying the denial of reality. As Murray (1986) remarks:

I think they were caught up with an unexamined assumption by this point of time, which was that the shuttle could be operational and everybody was doing his best to make what I think was a myth be true. . . . Not stupid, I think it was bad judgement . . . because the people were so under pressure and so blended into a mold that the shuttle was really a safe, reliable vehicle, that they no longer questioned that assumption. I think they stopped questioning that about four or five years earlier. (6–7)

Or, as the *New York Times* of 29 June 1986 reported:

"You've got to think it had everything to do with the shuttle going 'operational,' " said one investigator . . . In subtle ways, he continued, "NASA's top management 'conveyed the thought that it didn't want to hear about delays' that would further annoy Congress, which was already questioning why NASA had fallen behind its plan." (Business section, F8)

Thus, commitment to bad decisions leads to the denial of reality through self-idealization, which leads to further bad decisions, and so on.

Personnel Changes in Parallel with the Institutionalization of the Fiction

Advancement of Incompetent Individuals on the Basis of Ideology. As we saw in the previous chapter, to the extent that the core organizational process becomes the dramatization of the organization ideal, the standard for evaluation of individuals for promotion shifts from competence to ideological purity.

In government service, since the promotion system, especially at high levels, is controlled by individuals in the government itself, the relevant ideology is not so much the organization ideal, but the national ideology of the governing group. In this case the organization ideal is understood as a representation and example of this broader national ideology. Thus, partisan politics on the national level comes to be the determinant of promotability.

Trento (1987) provides evidence that the shift from competence to political suitability increasingly determined who would be promoted to top level administration at NASA. Consider this progression:

[James Beggs, NASA administrator under Reagan] spent a year at NASA under Webb. Beggs' wife Mary remembers Webb introducing them to President Johnson. "Jim was a Republican in NASA and they knew it. Jim Webb knew it. . . . He [Webb] said, 'I want you to know we look for people who can do the job in NASA, and we don't look for party affiliation,' " Mrs. Beggs remembers. (179–80)

But,

NASA was changing under Nixon. Paine agreed to accept political appointees to take over the NASA legal and legislative affairs offices. After that he found the White House pushing for more and more political appointees. (90)

And,

During the Nixon administration, people looking for political jobs had to be more than true-blue Republicans. They had to be Nixon loyalists. (96)

Then, with the advent of the Reagan administration, things went from bad to horrible. In the light of the idealization of business in Reagan's administration, consider what the following passage suggests about the reasons behind Beggs's choice:

[Former NASA Comptroller] Lilly described Beggs as a "nonentity" in his earlier stint at NASA. After all, to Lilly, Beggs was first and foremost a con-tractor. Unlike old NASA hands, Beggs believed that the contractor and gov-ernment were a partnership and not even occasionally adversaries. Such a rela-tionship was the ideal born out of a free-enterprise system and representative democracy. (184)

However,

Although he worked for Reagan's election, he was not one of the new, ultracon-servative Reaganite true believers. As a lifelong Republican businessman, Beggs did not realize that the conservatives' agenda was not subject to the kind of compromise that he was used to. If you were not one of them, you were against them. If Jim Beggs was an obstacle, he would be removed. (184)

And,

For all his experience in the corporate and political world, Jim Beggs was not prepared for the Reagan White House. He did not understand that appearance meant more than substance. That outward adherence to doctrinaire conservative philosophy meant more than the quality of the work. (253)

Indeed, Trento suggests that the sin that finally led to Beggs's removal, through the vehicle of a spurious indictment engineered by the Reagan administration, was that, while he was administrator, former radicals Jane Fonda and Tom Hayden were invited to a shuttle launch.

As the political criteria for NASA selection became more important,

Trento shows, the managerial and administrative competence of its high officials steadily decreased. The ultimate act in this tragedy came with the appointment of William R. Graham as Beggs's deputy, a position that led to his appointment as acting administrator eight days later, when Beggs was forced to take a leave of absence following his indictment.

Graham was forced on Beggs, who was tricked and browbeaten into taking him even though Graham's background was not in the space program but as a nuclear weapons expert, the largest group he had ever managed was twelve analysts at the RAND Corporation, Beggs, as he himself says, "had been warned by this time that the guy was a right-wing kook, a nut" (Trento 1987: 261), and NASA was under terrible pressure and the job of deputy administrator was no place for on-the-job training.

Since the explosion of the shuttle occurred only two months after his appointment as acting administrator, the fact of Graham's unsuitability for the top NASA post was not long in publicly emerging. He demonstrated that his knowledge of shuttle operations was deeply inadequate. This is from the *New York Times* of 3 February:

William R. Graham, Acting Administrator of the National Aeronautics and Space Administration, said that solid-fuel booster rockets were "some of the sturdiest parts of the entire shuttle system."

"They are considered primary structure, and not susceptible to failure," Dr. Graham said. . . .

Dr. Graham also said that, if there had been some warning, the seven member crew might have had time to attempt an emergency landing here at the Kennedy Space Center. (1)

All of these statements were false and would have been known to be false by anyone who had more than a passing acquaintance with NASA's operations. But Graham's lack of knowledge was at least partly due to his lack of experience. While regrettable, this would not necessarily have been his fault and conceivably could have been corrected if he had had the time.

What is much more disturbing was his apparent failure to recognize the limitations in his qualifications—a failure that would have precluded a serious attempt to correct these inadequacies. Thus, for example, when his name came from the White House as a candidate for the job, Beggs said that he had offered him another job in NASA that would be consistent with his qualifications. But, according to Beggs, Graham refused to take any other position. Again, on the day he took over from Beggs, according to Trento, "Graham . . . told a reporter, 'I'm in full charge and I intend to run this agency as though I am' " (272). This arrogance is what seems to me to be the fatal flaw here, both in Graham and in the system that promoted him to his position. Consider it in terms of the theory of the organization ideal.

Remember that the promotion system in the totalitarian organization is geared to advance individuals who idealize the organization. Then note that, as we have seen above, this idealization will be most pronounced toward those who most represent the organization: its highest officials (see Sievers 1986; and Klein and Ritti 1984: 170–72). Thus, Graham's arrogance may be understood as a natural concomitant, and even a requirement, of his high position in an organization like this. His position meant that he could, and even should, idealize himself and require that others do the same. He was, according to his ideology and the ideology of an increasingly totalitarian NASA, the ego ideal, and that meant to him that his ideological agenda was the meaning of NASA. Accordingly, at a time when NASA was burdened by perhaps the greatest degree of pressure that it had ever experienced, Beggs says:

"I did go about twice a week to pick up my mail and answer phone calls which were numerous. All the NASA people wanted to tell me what he [Graham] did today. The first thing he did was issue a lot of directives. He acted like a typical analyst. He sat in his office with the door closed and wrote directives. The first directive he wrote described how you were supposed to wear your NASA badge. The second directive he wrote was a standards of conduct memo on what was permissible and what was not permissible for NASA employees." (quoted in Trento 1987: 277)

As Trento reports:

Beggs, Kennedy Space Center Director Dick Smith, and others remember that Graham was very concerned about the guest list for the 51-L launch. Beggs said he received a phone call a few days before the scheduled launch of 51-L from the Public Affairs Office. "They said, 'What's with this guy Graham?' And I said, 'I don't know. What's he doing now?' And they said, 'Well he is reviewing in detail the whole guest list.' And I said, 'What's he doing?' Well he [the Public Affairs Officer] says, 'He's [Graham's] scratching names out he says he is going to get in trouble with on the HIll.' " The public affairs people told Beggs that

Graham was taking Democrats and any others he perceived to have liberal leanings off the list. (282)

Discouragement and Alienation of Competent Individuals. Another result of the selection of incompetent individuals is that realistic and competent persons who are committed to their work lose the belief that the organization's real purpose is productive work and come to the conclusion that its real purpose is self-idealization. They then are likely to see their work as being alien to the purposes of the organization. Some will withdraw from the organization psychologically. Others will buy into the nonsense around them, cynically or through self-deception (Goffman 1959), and abandon their concern with reality. Still others will conclude that the only way to save their self-esteem is to leave the organization. Arguably, it is these last individuals who, because of their commitment to productive work and their firm grasp of reality, are the most productive members of the organization.

Trento (1987) cites a number of instances of this happening at NASA. His account of the disillusionment of Rocco Petrone is typical:

In the terrible place that NASA became in the years after Apollo, there was someone who tried to stop the headlong rush to disaster. There was a man who stood up to Dale Myers and George Low and even James Fletcher and said you cannot do this. You cannot abandon everything learned about management in Apollo to build the shuttle on the cheap. Rocco Petrone was a lone voice. And that is why he quit NASA in 1975. He did not want to participate in what he believed to be a combination of self-delusion and lies to sell the shuttle. He was in charge of manned spaceflight for NASA, yet this West Point man found himself with less and less influence over a program he was supposed to be running. (238)

Petrone argued against taking paperwork and management shortcuts. Petrone told his superiors that the one thing NASA learned from Apollo was that accountability led to success. As they found out in the Apollo 204 fire, to remove that accountability could be a fatal error. Yet, to save money, that is exactly the road NASA management selected. Petrone argued that Low and Fletcher were wrong when they said no escape system existed on airplanes and therefore the shuttle did not need one. Because of the success in NASA's track record, Petrone argued that Americans would have great difficulty accepting the loss of astronauts. He said that Americans would not accept astronauts dying. He told them they had to have as escape system. Petrone brought in outside experts to look at the shuttle system. Their findings confirmed his views for the record. Then he left NASA. (239)

The Narcissistic Loss of Reality among Management

As we saw exemplified in the case of William Graham, management in the totalitarian organization comes to believe that it has attained its goal of becoming again the center of a loving world. It takes itself to be the ego ideal and insists that it be taken as such by subordinates, even to the extent that information that conflicts with management's overvaluation of itself will be withheld. This is the case with information concerning the state of the environment, but it is true as well about information concerning the internal state of the organization.

Thus, subordinates will know that their security and advancement depend on the success of their portrayal of the organization as the organization ideal: of its management as perfect management and of themselves as perfectly integrated employees. Given their need to believe in the organization ideal and as part of the cultural transformation, they may even repress their own perceptions to believe this. Whether they believe in the organization ideal or not, their dramatization of it will further decrease management's hold on reality and render it and the organization increasingly ineffective. This in turn will increase the demands on the subordinates to assist management in divorcing itself from reality. This narcissistic state of NASA management was revealed in its response to the Cook memorandum.

Richard C. Cook, a budget analyst for NASA, was assigned to assess the impact of any problems with the SRBs. In a memorandum written on 23 July 1985, he warned that flight safety was being compromised by erosion of the seal O-rings and that failure would be catastrophic. After the explosion, he wrote another memo, referring back to his first, which was leaked to the Rogers Commission, who called him to testify on 12 February. Cook claimed that his information was based solely on what the engineers working on the SRBs had told him, but the Rogers Commission was dismissive and called NASA witnesses to refute his charges. In evaluating their response, recall that this was before it had been established that the O-rings were, in fact, the problem.

ROGERS: Ah, it's fair then to say that after or at about the same time Mr. Cook's memorandum was written in July, 85, that you and your team were, had been and were at that time conducting a lot of investigations, doing a lot of work about the O-rings.

[DAVID] WINTERHALTER [acting director of NASA's shuttle propulsion division]: That's correct, sir.

ROGERS: But in the final analysis, the qualified people, the engineers and others who were assigned responsibility of their decisions have to make the decisions.

WINTERHALTER: That's true. And I pride, I prided myself on our division to be particularly good team workers. We have our differences, we work 'em out. . . . At no time . . . during that period did any of my people come to me, give any indication that they felt like there was any, any safety of flight problems in their area.

Q: Was it the view of your division, the propulsion group, that the seal design, as it was installed and operating in the shuttle system was ah, safe and adequate?

WINTERHALTER: It was. (*New York Times,* 13 February 1986: B11)

The *Times* went on to say that a "parade" of NASA officials testified that Mr. Cook's concerns were out of proportion and that the issue of seal erosion had been dealt with carefully by NASA engineering experts and managers. They said that seal problems had diminished in 1985.[2] Cook's boss, Michael B. Mann, said he checked with the engineers and concluded that "maybe the memo overstated their concerns." While the NASA officials did not deny Cook's assertion that seals had eroded, they did claim that more competent professionals than he had concluded they were safe.

The next day, the *Times* gave Cook a chance to respond. In evaluating his interpretation, bear in mind that, as subsequent investigation has shown, he was entirely correct in his apprehensions:

In his first major interview since publication of his internal memorandum, . . . Richard C. Cook, said that propulsion engineers at the National Aeronautics and Space Administration "whispered" in his ear ever since he arrived last July that the seals were unsafe and even "held their breath" when earlier shuttles were launched.

But he said such concerns got submerged because the "whole culture of the place" calls for a "can-do attitude that NASA can do what ever it tries to do, can solve any problem that comes up" as it "roars ahead toward 24 shuttle flights a year."

And,

Mr. Cook said he based his warning memorandum last July on conversations with engineers in the agency's propulsion division who were concerned about erosion of the rocket's safety seals. "They began to tell me that some of these things were being eaten away," he said, "and rather innocently I asked what does that mean?"

"They said to me, almost in a whisper in my ear, that the thing could blow up," he continued. "I was shocked." In his July memorandum, Mr. Cook explained, "I was simply paraphrasing what this engineering group was telling me. I was not making it up that flight safety was being compromised and the results could be catastrophic. I didn't put it in my memorandum, but one of them said to me, 'When this thing goes up, we hold our breath.' "

Cook went on to give his opinion of how this blockage of information takes place. In a scenario that will be familiar from the last chapter, he pointed toward the pressure felt by lower personnel to support the image of organizational infallibility:

Cook said that, in meetings called by the shuttle program managers, a middle-level engineer with safety concerns is "just a little guy."

"You aren't going to find an engineer with 20 years' experience and a livelihood to protect stand up and say, 'Excuse me, but we might have an explosion on the next shuttle flight because the O-rings might break. It's just not going to happen.'

"If some did get up, he would quickly be branded a nay-sayer," Mr. Cook said. "I never said a word in these meetings. I was a nobody, more junior than the veteran engineers. And there is always the nagging thought in the engineers' minds that, 'Gee, we may be wrong. Maybe nothing will happen.' " (14 February 1986, B4)

Again, it is fascinating to see how blind NASA officials were to this constriction, which was evidently common knowledge to everyone else, and how confident they were that things were as they were supposed to be:

Today, L. Michael Weeks, deputy associate Administrator for space flight, the space agency's second-ranking shuttle official, said that the climate at the agency actually encouraged individuals two or three levels below him to speak their minds on safety concerns. He said that working-level engineers "don't hesitate to tell Mike Weeks anything" and "quite often will argue right on the spot at a significant meeting with me or with Jesse," a reference to Jesse W. Moore, the top shuttle official. (14 February 1986, B4)

Feynman's Test

The detachment of NASA management from reality offers a way to introduce a concept that may be thought of as a test for systemic organizational decay. I call it *Feynman's test*.

Commissioner Richard P. Feynman grew bored with some of the irrelevant detail that he thought he was being subjected to, so, as he says, "I made up a little game for myself": [3]

Imagine that something else had failed—the main engines, for instance—and we were making the same kind of intensive investigation as we are now: would we discover the same slipping safety criteria and lack of communication? (Feynman 1989: 181)

He began his own investigation of the main rocket engines by asking to talk to a few engineers who worked with them. They got together with him, as did their supervisor, Mr. Lovingood. Feynman began to focus on the question of what their estimate of the reliability of the main engines would be, curious as to whether they would come up with the same wildly unrealistic estimates of reliability that NASA had claimed for the shuttle system itself.

In the course of the briefing he asked the engineers and Lovingood to write down their estimates of the reliability of the main engines. The estimates of the engineers ranged from 1 in 200 to 1 in 300. Lovingood waffled, but when pressed came up with the same figure NASA gave for the total system, 1 in 100,000. This suggested to Feynman that the same managerial isolation from reality was at work here as in the case of the SRB components. [4]

Feynman went on to talk with the engineers and Lovingood about other technical matters concerning the main engines. On the basis of the discussion he came to this conclusion:

When I left the meeting, I had the definite impression that I had found the same game as with the seals: management reducing criteria and accepting more and more errors that weren't designed into the device, while the engineers are screaming from below, "HELP!" and "This is a RED ALERT!" (185)

CONCLUSION

NASA was, thus, a decadent organization. Next, I will show how its narcissistic processes led to the decision to launch the *Challenger*.

6

On the Psychodynamics of Organizational Disaster: The Case of the Space Shuttle *Challenger*

That NASA became a decadent organization, an organization that had abandoned reality for fantasy, provides a perfectly adequate explanation for the *Challenger* disaster. The physical world is not an "enacted environment" (Weick 1977). It is not the external dramatization of our wishes and whims. On the contrary, it possesses a resilience and recalcitrance that will mock the dreamer. An organization like NASA, whose business involves dealing with physical reality, has only a very limited margin in which it can indulge itself in fantasy before disaster becomes inevitable. I wish now to show how the decision to launch *Challenger* emerged from this indulgence in fantasy.

The most important key to the understanding of the *Challenger* disaster lies in what I have called ontological differentiation, which, again, involves a twofold fantasy. First is the fantasy of the perfection of the organization, of the organization as the center of creation. Second is the fantasy that high officials of the organization are embodiments of this perfection since they embody the organization.

With regard to this second fantasy, it may be worthwhile to observe again that, for the powerful, the fantasy of their perfection invokes a great temptation toward rejecting any who do not conform to the story. It was after all, the pursuit of perfection that committed these participants to the organization in the first place. In this way, organizational power becomes enlisted in the process of fantasy.

NASA AND THE ORGANIZATION IDEAL

This part of the chapter will show how the psychology of the organization ideal led to the explosion of the space shuttle.

Technological Russian Roulette

According to Rogers Commission member Richard P. Feynman, NASA officials were playing a strange game of Russian roulette. Here is the account as given in the *New York Times* of 4 April:

> Dr. Feynman . . . said that typically in flight readiness reviews, conducted a week or two before launchings, space agency officials would "agonize whether they can go" even though the seals may have eroded on the previous flight. But then, if they decided to launch and the flight occurred safely, he said, on the next flight they lowered their standards a bit because they "got away with it the last time." He described the process as "a kind of Russian roulette" or a "perpetual movement heading for trouble."

Putting the matter in terms of probability brings out Feynman's point most clearly. In the case of Russian roulette, with one round in the cylinder, the odds are one in six that a pull on the trigger will fire the round. If the round does not fire on the first pull, and the cylinder is spun, the odds are again one in six for the next pull on the trigger. To some persons unfamiliar with theories of probability, it may seem that the odds with each successive pull would be greater. This is, of course, wrong. But it is equally wrong to suppose that the odds will be less with each successive event. This, however, is what the NASA officials appeared to believe. The question is, how can it have happened that NASA officials, knowing full well the laws of probability, could have made such an error?

My answer is that NASA officials were engaged in the calculation of two very different sorts of probabilities. Both calculations were legitimate within their domains. The problem is that one of the domains existed only in fantasy.

One calculation was an engineering calculation. Given what is known of the technology, it is possible to estimate roughly the degree of risk involved. It is probable though, that the calculation was distorted by the other sort of calculation, which I call the attribution of agency.

In order to understand the idea of the attribution of agency, it is necessary to return to the concept of the organization ideal. As we know, the organization ideal is an image of perfection. It is, so to speak, an idea of a god. God does not make mistakes. Having adopted the idea of NASA as the organization ideal, the individual will believe that, if NASA has made a decision, that decision will be correct. I will refer to decisions made by NASA, considered as the organization ideal, as NASA decisions. In the case of NASA decisions, NASA may be said to "work through" NASA employees. However, there would be another type of decision within the NASA frame of interaction. As we saw, narcissism does not return to the individual in reality, and individuals recognizing this must know that they and their colleagues are not perfect. Maintaining a belief in the ideal character of NASA, these people can say of themselves and their colleagues that they are not fully NASA, even though the possibility exists that some day they may be. Hence, if these mortals, these people who are within the NASA organization but are not NASA, made the decision, it will be a different sort of decision. Call it a human decision. Human decisions, unlike NASA decisions, are fallible.

Now, given a decision within the NASA frame of interaction, the question becomes is it a NASA decision or a human decision? Specifically, was the complex decision involved in the design and construction of the SRB seals a NASA decision or a human decision? If it was a human decision, engineering standards of risk should have prevailed in determining whether the shuttle was safe to launch. On the other hand, if the decision was a NASA decision, the reasoning there was simply that the *Challenger* was safe to launch, since NASA does not make mistakes. If I believe in NASA decisions, the first question I ask is whether a decision is a NASA decision, because if it is, I don't have to worry about the engineering probabilities at all. And here the history of success is related to the determination of probability. For, since NASA decisions are infallible, every instance of a given decision being correct provides evidence that the decision was a NASA decision. Thus, in this question, it makes perfectly good sense to decrease the probability of failure with each successful launch.

Why the Question Concerning the Effects of Cold on the Seals Was Not Passed Up the Chain of Command

When the Rogers Commission ([RC] 1986) determined that the decision-making process at NASA was flawed, what they specifically had in mind was that the questions raised by Morton-Thiokol engineers concerning the effects of cold weather on the SRB seals were discussed at a relatively low level (Level III) and not passed up higher to Level II or I. It appears that a major moving force in determining that the question not be transmitted upward was Lawrence Mulloy, SRB project manager at the Marshall Space Flight Center. The retrospective reasoning in Mulloy's testimony is interesting:

MR. MULLOY: . . . I did not discuss with Mr. Aldrich [National Space Transportation Program manager] the conversations that we had just completed with Morton-Thiokol.

CHAIRMAN ROGERS: Could you explain why?

MR. MULLOY: Yes, sir. At that time, and I still consider today, that was a Level III issue, Level III being an SRB element or an external tank element or Space Shuttle main engine element or an Orbiter. There was no violation of Launch Commit Criteria. There was no waiver required in my judgment at that time and still today.

And we work many problems at the Orbiter and the SRB and the External Tank level that never get communicated to Mr. Aldrich or Mr. Moore [associate administrator for space flight]. It was clearly a Level III issue that had been resolved. (RC: 98)

From one point of view Mulloy's reasoning makes perfectly good sense. It was up to him, and his Level III colleagues, to decide whether the specific elements in question were flightworthy. We have to place this reasoning, however, against the fact that the discussion concerning the effects of cold on the seals had been heated and even acrimonious, and that even after the matter had been formally resolved, Allan McDonald, manager of the Morton-Thiokol Space Booster Project and Morton-Thiokol representative at the Kennedy Space Center, continued to argue vehemently against the launch. The point is that, while in the formal sense, Level III had the authority to rule the SRB flightworthy, they also had the authority to pass questions on to Levels II and I, which, of course had authority over the whole system. From this point of view, Mulloy's justification is simply a non-sequitur.

The real issue was posed by a television commentator (George F. Will, I believe) who was incredulous that anyone in an organization would take this much risk upon her- or himself, when everything we know about organizations suggests that the most natural thing to do is to pass it on. There is an additional element that makes the question even more interesting from an organizational point of view. It is that Mulloy justified his decision on the basis of the fact that there was no Launch Commit Criteron that took account of temperature and therefore none that forbade the launch. In other words, Mulloy rests his defense on the fact that he was following the rules, which is certainly a familiar enough organizational defense. But typically, in an organization, participants follow rules to keep themselves out of trouble. Mulloy, by contrast, appeared to follow a rule that could get him into trouble— not to reduce his risk but to increase it. He did so, as we have seen, in a perfectly gratuitous fashion.

These facts make sense from the standpoint of the theory of the organization ideal. If, for the committed participant, the organization represents the ego ideal, then participation in the organization's successful activity is a route to narcissism. Accordingly, there is a built-in tendency to take responsibility and to exercise that responsibility with a bias for positive action. The organization's achievements, after all, are realized only through positive action. Thus, taking responsibility for positive action is a way of linking "I did it" with the "NASA did it" that represents perfection.

Moreover, similar considerations in fact mitigate against taking problems to a higher level. The pursuit of narcissism through the participation in the organization is, as we have seen, linked to movement through the hierarchy and entails the assumption that the most perfect union of individual and organization occurs at the top. It is for this reason that those lower down in the organization feel it incumbent upon themselves to play out the drama of the return to narcissism of those higher up. Characteristic of the return to narcissism is the experience of everything being right and perfect. By keeping problems at a lower level, therefore, Mulloy and his colleagues were not only opting for their share of participation in NASA perfection, but reinforcing the drama of perfection by dramatizing to their superiors that everything was just fine and that NASA was moving along in its inexorably perfect way.

Nonetheless, as we have seen, the return to narcissism is only an illusion, and while Mulloy and his colleagues can believe in that illusion with respect to their superiors and in fact help to build the very illusion that they come to believe in, their own experience may contain the seeds of doubt. For, if the perfect linkage of individual and organization is fantasized to occur at the top of the organization, this implies that, lower down, the linkage may be incomplete. There may have been other factors also. Perhaps the argument with Morton-Thiokol engineers had some impact. Here is where we see the importance of the rules. The rules of NASA, in this case the Launch Commit Criteria, represent its procedural body. In following them, Mulloy and his colleagues could touch, as it were, a bit of the living flesh of NASA and assure themselves of the success of their venture.

The Reduction of Process to Ritual

The emphasis placed by Mulloy and his colleagues on the Launch Commit Criteria may be put in the context of a more general approach to NASA procedures that exemplifies the transformation of once vital organizational processes into empty rituals (see chapter 4).

Some evidence suggests that twenty years ago NASA was a model organization not only in terms of its engineering achievement but in terms of its organizational characteristics. Indeed, the NASA of twenty years ago appears to have been a perfect instantiation of the sort of openly communicating, organic, nonhierarchical organization that theorists like McGregor (1960), Argyris (1964), and Likert (1961) recommended.

The odd thing about NASA is that, in large measure, the procedures that represented these organic processes appear to have remained in place. Thus, NASA and contractor engineers certainly had the right to question the safety of the shuttle, and, in fact, they did so. The problem was that their concerns did not register as important in the minds of NASA management.

Perhaps the most tragic example of this condition was the way the objections of engineers to the SRB seals—a series of objections that began in 1977 (RC 1986:122), four years before the first shuttle flight, and never ended—were disregarded by NASA management. But there are other instances of management's obliviousness. Consider, for example, testimony describing the way NASA treated the concerns of Rockwell officials about the safety of flying in icy conditions. The *New York Times* reported:

Robert Glaysher, a Rockwell vice president, reading from notes at the time, said he had explicitly told launching officials, "Rockwell can not assure that it is safe to fly." . . . he testified that Rockwell's position was equivalent to saying it was "unsafe to fly." (28 February 1986: D19)

And, the article notes:

Somehow, the message never got across. Arnold Aldrich, the No. 2 man in the shuttle program, said that he thought Rockwell was expressing "concerns," but that he would have never authorized a launching if the prime contractor had objected. Mr Aldrich said that, to his mind, "they did not intend to ask me not to launch."

Several commission members said that they were puzzled how a recommendation against launching could be mysteriously translated into a cautious recommendation in favor.

The behavior of NASA management again makes sense from the standpoint of the theory of the organization ideal. Management and employees hold an article of faith that NASA, proceeding according to its essential movement, makes infallible decisions. To the extent that NASA managers are operating under the assumption of being NASA, and to the extent that the form of NASA's decision-making is followed, they think of their decisions as being infallible. As long, therefore, as managers "listened to the concerns" of engineers and contractors, the success of the venture would be assured.

The problem is that while the image of NASA making infallible decisions is part of the culture of NASA for its managers, that image provides no guidance in the making of decisions and does not in any way insure that the specific decision will be correct. In fact, once the assumption of infallibility is made, it may even degrade the quality of decisions by impeding the serious and self-critical consideration of criticisms and alternatives. Ironically, this holds true even if the criticisms and alternatives are already in the system, since they can now be ignored on the grounds that they were formally "listened to" before.

What becomes clear is that while the form of decision-making may remain the same, its content becomes free to vary; and to the extent that the form is relied upon as a guarantee of success, the content can become completely arbitrary.

The Disappearance of Pressure

The scenario that popular consciousness has developed for explaining the disaster makes a particular appeal to the concept of pressure. NASA was under pressure from Congress, from the president, from the news media, and so on, and so, naturally, it overextended itself and tried to do more than it could. I have no doubt that this is true. What strikes me as peculiar is the remarkable unanimity with which NASA officials denied that they were responding to pressure or, for that matter, were passing on this pressure to anyone else.

From an organizational standpoint, what is remarkable about NASA management's stance is that the claim that they were responding to pressure would have taken at least some of the heat off NASA and put it on the entities that were applying the pressure. But, strikingly, they did not take this way out and remained insistent that the decisions that they had made were the correct decisions, occasioned by their own sober and professional assessment of the situation. A phenomenon of this sort simply begs for an explanation outside of the ordinary.

From the standpoint of the theory of the organization ideal, pressure is not apprehended because it is inconsistent with the idea of the organization as an ideal. The organization ideal does not move because it is pressed to move. On the contrary, being pressed to move is a characteristic of the finite, limited, vulnerable side of our individual existences, which the idea of the organization ideal is constructed to deny. Thus, the organization ideal moves because of its own internal causes. It is the cause of itself—in the old medieval expression, *causa sui*. Moreover, the organization does not need to put pressure on anything or anybody else. All it needs to do is to make its vision clear to others, and, if they have intelligence and good will, they will naturally agree. The reason for this ready compliance again goes back to the conception of the organization ideal as a project for the return to narcissism. The world is a loving world of which the organization is center. All the organization needs to do is be itself, and the world will naturally fall into line. There is no need to put pressure on it.

The phenomenon of the organization's being blind to the pressure it has caused is evident in the critical 27 January teleconference between NASA Level III management and Morton-Thiokol. In the course of this teleconference, Morton-Thiokol made it clear to NASA management that they recommended against the launch because of the effects cold might have on the SRB O-rings. The discussion became a heated one. Lawrence Mulloy said that he did not accept the recommendation and asked if Morton-Thiokol wanted him to wait until April to launch. At the same time, George Hardy, deputy director of science and engineering, said he would not launch against Morton-Thiokol's recommendation, but that he was "appalled" that they would make such a recommendation.

At this point, Morton-Thiokol management asked to go off the teleconference loop while they reconsidered the recommendation. When they came back on, as the result of processes that may be signified by Robert Lund, vice president of engineering, "taking off his engineering hat and putting on his management hat," and despite the fact that there was not one engineer who recommended the launch, Morton-Thiokol management had been able to change their assessment and had come to approve the launch. Even so, when they sent their written approval, the letter still brought up the engineering grounds upon which Morton-Thiokol had previously recommended against launch.

Now it seems to me that anyone who was in the least bit sensitive to the pressure he or she was causing would have known that this was a situation in which pressure had been exerted. But the Level III management involved showed no sign whatsoever that they knew that they had exerted pressure. This point is made repeatedly in their testimony (*New York Times*, 26–28 February 1986), and it also manifested itself behaviorally. If NASA Level III knew that it had exerted pressure, and therefore that the resolution had been political, they would have known that the safety question had not been resolved on an engineering basis, and therefore they would have been worried about the safety of the flight. But they showed no signs of having been worried. Thus, Mulloy and Reinartz mentioned to William Lucas, Marshall Center director, that Morton-Thiokol had raised concerns about the seals, but they mentioned it in such a way that Lucas had no impression that the matter had not been entirely resolved. Again, Mulloy and Reinhartz sat for several hours with Aldrich and Moore before the launch without ever mentioning that there had been a disagreement.

Perhaps the fact that the 27 January teleconference was the most minutely investigated element of the disaster is the reason that it also gives us the best example of what the denial of pressure looks like with regard to the people who are being pressured. For, it is clear that, on the one hand, Morton-Thiokol was under considerable pressure to please an important customer and go along with NASA's desire to launch, while, on the other hand, it appears that this pressure was not regarded by Morton-Thiokol management, as opposed to Morton-Thiokol engineers, as pressure at the time, nor remembered as pressure by them. Thus, engineers Allan McDonald and Brian Russell, as well as other Morton-Thiokol engineers, testified that they had felt pressure, but Jerry

Mason, senior vice president, said: "There was some pressure, but I believe it was in the range of what we normally encounter," and Joe Kilminster, vice president for shuttle projects, said, "I did not feel a significant amount of pressure" to change position (*New York Times*, 26 February 1986).

Evidently, the differentiation coincided with a disparity in perception of the way that NASA had redefined the situation, from one in which they had to prove that it was safe to fly, to one in which they had to prove it was unsafe to fly. Morton-Thiokol engineers evidently realized that the situation was being redefined, while management did not. Thus, Robert Lunden said:

"We have always dealt with Marshall for a long time and have always been in the position of defending our position to make sure that we were ready to fly, and I guess I didn't realize until after the meeting and after several days that we had absolutely changed our position from what we had before." (RC1986:94)

It appears that we have here, in the case of Morton-Thiokol management, an example of the dynamics Freud (1955) associated with leadership. For Freud, the leader takes the place of the follower's ego ideal. In the process, the individual's sense of judgment, his or her reflecting, critical ability, is given over to the leader, and consequently the individual's sense of moral autonomy is lost. With regard to the Morton-Thiokol engineers, this had not happened, or at least not completely. This is why the Morton-Thiokol engineers felt pressure, while the managers did not. The experience of pressure involves a sense of oneself as a distinct entity against another distinct entity. Thus the engineers maintained a sense of their authority by retaining their own ego ideal—an ego ideal in which their professional engineering standards played a large part.[1] For the managers, however, putting NASA in the place of their ego ideal meant, in effect, that they had taken NASA as their image of what they should be themselves, the realization of their own narcissism. In this way, the boundaries between them and NASA vanished. They fused with NASA and gave up their sense of being distinct entities. In effect, these people had given up their own selves. There was no self that could have experienced pressure.

Similar considerations apply to the question of why the engineers felt that the situation had been redefined to require proof of why it was dangerous to launch. This is a question that makes sense only if the issue being discussed is one of launch safety—an engineering issue. But for management, this does not appear to have been the question. The institutional question, the management issue, as they saw it, was how to please NASA, how to confirm NASA's narcissism, and while the details may have shifted, the primary task remained the same. Hence, when Bob Lund "Took off his engineer's hat and put on his manager's hat," the issue for him was already decided. Indeed, once Mason announced that a "management decision" would have to be made, the issue was already decided and further disagreement on engineering grounds became irrelevant. Engineers Roger Boisjoly and Arnold Thompson came to recognize that once the management orientation had been adopted, the discussion was over and the engineering question had become irrelevant. Boisjoly's testimony is useful in providing a sense of how this recognition felt:

"Okay, the caucus started by Mr. Mason stating a management decision was necessary. Those of us who opposed the launch continued to speak out . . . And we were attempting to go back and rereview and try to make clear what we were trying to get across, and we couldn't understand why it was going to be reversed. So we spoke out and tried to explain once again the effects of low temperature. Arnie actually got up from his position which was down the table, and walked up to the table and put a quarter pad down in front of the table, in front of the management folks, and tried to sketch once again what his concern was with the joint, and when he realized he wasn't getting through, he just stopped.

"I tried once more with the photos. I grabbed the photos, and I went up and discussed the photos once again and tried to make the point that it was my opinion from actual observations that temperature was indeed a discriminator and we should not ignore the physical evidence that we had observed . . . I also stopped when it was apparent that I couldn't get anybody to listen." (RC 1986:92)

The Denial of Disaster

Often, the organization manages to respond to external pressures while still maintaining the idea of itself as *causa sui* by generating a fantasy that rationalizes the actions it is being forced to take in a way that still leaves it with the concept of its own control. Thus, in a classic study, Festinger, Riecken, and Schacter (1956) observed what happened to a sect that had predicted the end of the world at a specific time. As that time approached, and nothing happened, there was a revelation: The world had been spared as a result of the sect's activities, and the sect was then charged with the responsibility of preaching this good news.

In the case of NASA, as we have seen, the dominant fantasy had been the fantasy of NASA's infallibility, subject to its forms and rituals being followed. If the forms were followed, success was assured, and it then became the responsibility of critics to prove that NASA should not act, rather than for them to prove that it should. This is clear in the testimony of Morton-Thiokol engineers.

It seems to me to be this flight into fantasy that was responsible for the most remarkable aspect of the public testimony concerning the disaster—NASA management's apparent belief that they made the right decision. The only way this belief could be maintained was by supposing that making the right decision meant making the decision in the right way, regardless of consequences. This was the impression many of these NASA managers gave. Thus, to cite only one example, William Lucas said: "I'm not sure what Mr. Rogers means in terms of the decision process being flawed" (*This Week with David Brinkley*, 8 June 1986). The differentiation between NASA management's infallibility fantasy and reality was sufficiently jarring to become a focus of public discussion. Thus, according to the *New York Times* of 17 March 1986:

One Marshall manager confided that he was embarrassed to hear the center's officials contending that the decision making process leading to the launching was "sound."

"The shuttle blew up and you had pieces falling from the sky," he noted. "How could it not be flawed?"

REORGANIZING NASA

In response to the *Challenger* disaster and as general schemes for averting disaster, two general strategies were put forward as ways of reorganizing NASA. First was what may be called the solution through structure. Change the organization's structure in some way, it was proposed, and the problems would be taken care of. This was the basic solution that the Rogers Commission recommended. There should be more central accountability, the program manager should have more authority, astronauts should be in management, there should be a shuttle safety panel, and so on and so forth. The problem with programs like these is not that they are not desirable, at least in the short run, but that they do not address the central issue, and therefore, in the long run, they run the risk of becoming part of the problem. I have discussed this already with regard to the fact that vital organizational processes tend to become ritualized.

Actually, I suspect that such recommendations are often intended not so much as offering real solutions to problems, but as excuses for avoiding problems. This is a conclusion that can be supported by Feynman's (1989) observations with regard to the Rogers Commission recommendations:

> Sometime in May, at one of our last meetings, we got around to making a list of possible recommendations. Somebody would say, "Maybe one of the things we should discuss is the establishment of a safety board."
> "Okay, we'll put that down."
> I'm thinking, "At last! We're going to have a discussion!"
> But it turns out that this tentative list of topics *becomes* the recommendations —that there be a safety board, that there be a this, that there be a that. The only discussion was about which recommendation we should write first, which one should come second, and so forth.
> There were many things I wanted to discuss further. For example, in regard to a safety board, one could ask: "Wouldn't such a committee just add another layer to an already overgrown bureaucracy?"
> There had been safety boards before. In 1967, after the Apollo accident, the investigating committee at the time invented a special panel for safety. It worked for a while, but it didn't last.
> We didn't discuss why the earlier safety boards were no longer effective; instead, we just made up more safety boards. (199)

The second possibility may be called the solution through culture. The *New York Times* of 10 June 1986 reported:

> Some senior NASA officials have conceded that as much as changing personnel, the agency needs to instill a new "culture" in which lower-level managers and engineers feel freer to communicate "bad news," such as the poor O-ring performance, to key decision makers. They said such a culture existed during the Apollo project, which was clearly defined as a research and development undertaking and in which problem-solving was an accepted part of the process. (22)

The difficulty with this approach is that, as regards NASA management at least—and of course they would be the ones who would be charged with "instilling" a new culture—NASA's culture was already fine. In the case of communicating bad news, for example, numerous NASA managers testified repeatedly that this was part of the NASA culture. The only problem was that while it may have been part of NASA "culture," in the sense of the way in which NASA management saw and understood its activities, this "culture" had no relationship to the truth.

We saw this above in NASA management's response to the Cook memorandum, but it was also evident in the case of NASA's concern for safety. Public statements of NASA officials so often stressed NASA's concern for safety that if one did not know about the explosion of the space shuttle, one could never have suspected that it happened. But at the time that this supposedly safety-conscious NASA was acting to make sure that no unnecessary risk could take place, they were cutting their safety budget by half a billion dollars (*New York Times,* 24 April 1986) and their quality control staff by 70 percent (*New York Times,* 8 May 1986).

Argyris and Schön (1974) refer to the way that an organization's culture can be unrelated to its reality by distinguishing between a manager's espoused theory and his or her theory-in-use. They point out that one does not typically have any relationship to the other. The theory of the organization ideal provides a complementary perspective. Here, the organization's culture provides the framework within which the actions of those in power are justified. From this point of view, what the specific culture is, is of secondary significance. What is important is that organizational participants, both lower and, especially, upper, have a stake in seeing that the justificatory process takes place, no matter what the facts are. This is the point at which fantasy gains the upper hand. The idea of bringing reality back in by changing the content of the fantasy is, of course, absurd.

On Averting Organizational Disasters

It becomes clear that seeing organizational disasters from the standpoint of the theory of the organization ideal—as a natural by-product of organizational decay[2]—poses a serious problem for the organization that is concerned to prevent them. If a disaster is the product of a flawed organizational process within an organizational context that is healthy, then it is at least conceivable that the process can be changed to avert further disasters of the same sort. On the other hand, if the disaster is the result of systemic decay, its cause cannot be isolated within a specific area of organizational functioning and repaired therein. Moreover, the very means that are required in the repair of an organizational process

—such as feedback, problem identification, even reflexive action of the organization upon itself—are likely to be as much in decay as the original problematic process. Preventing the occurrence and recurrence of disasters, to the extent that they are caused by organizational decay, requires an organizational strategy of a different sort. Indeed, it requires an organizational strategy that is not even an organizational strategy.

Organizational decay is the result of a denial of reality and a concomitant addiction to fantasy. The reality that is denied is the reality of the individual's separation, limitation, and mortality. It seems inevitable that the solution to the problem of organizational decay must involve the acceptance of this reality.

Within this context, the idea of a solution to organizational decay does not look like a specific program that powerful administrators can impose on and through a powerful, potentially perfect organization. Rather, it comes to look like a group of limited men and women, trying hard each day to reclaim, within the terrible constraints that each one faces, a little bit of the hold on reality that each one, him- or herself, threw away. This is a matter to which I shall return in the concluding chapter.

Part Three

AMERICAN CULTURE AND THE *CHALLENGER* DISASTER: A HISTORICAL PERSPECTIVE

7

The Symbol of the Space Shuttle and the
Degeneration of the American Dream

In the South Seas there is a cargo cult of people. During the war they saw airplanes land with lots of good materials, and they want the same thing to happen now. So they've arranged to make things like runways, to put fires along the sides of the runways, to make a wooden hut for a man to sit in, with two wooden pieces on his head like headphones and bars of bamboo sticking out like antennas—he's the controller—and they wait for the airplanes to land. They're doing everything right. The form is perfect. It looks exactly the way it looked before. But it doesn't work. No airplanes land.
—Richard P. Feynman,
Surely You're Joking, Mr. Feynman

I am looking at a photograph. Seven smiling people look back at me. Five of them are men, two are women; five are white, one is black, one is Oriental. Of the men, two look boyish, one is gray haired and looks older than the rest. They are all dressed in identical coveralls that give no hint at all of the specific characteristics of their bodies. Each coverall has the NASA logo on it. On the table next to them is a model of a space shuttle. Behind them is an American flag. They will be the crew of the space shuttle *Challenger*, flight 51-L.

My imagination takes me past this picture. I see them in space. They cavort weightlessly. They point television cameras out the window and show me how Earth looks from space. Through the marvel of television, I am there with them in the space shuttle, in space. All Americans were with them in space. Even the children are there. For one of these astronauts is a teacher who will conduct classes in space.

There is a feeling of completeness that comes to me with this vision. It is as if my imagination has gone beyond the reconfiguration of common perceptual elements and has entered the realm of the mythic. The picture sings to me: look what America has done! America has transcended its cleavages, men and women fly together, the races fly together, the ages fly together. Even the children can fly. We are all up there in a machine that manages to be, at the same time, powerful and thrusting, like a phallus, and warm and comforting, like a womb. Earthly cares are overcome. Earth and care are overcome. There are no limits to what Americans can do. Constraint is merely an illusion. I feel on the edge of immortality itself.

I wrote these words in June 1986, as part of a proposal for an academic conference. What I did not know at the time was that the image that came to me from the picture was the image that was supposed to have come to me. As I shall show later, what I had thought of as a spontaneous and creative act of my autonomous imagination was actually the result of a conscious, carefully crafted process of symbol creation that was geared to produce this effect. I was picking up the image of itself that NASA was transmitting.

As Geertz (1973) has observed in his analysis of the Balinese cockfight, through some of their institutions, societies talk to themselves about themselves. Thus:

> Like any art form—for that, finally, is what we are dealing with—the cockfight renders ordinary, everyday experience comprehensible by presenting it in terms of acts and objects which have had their practical consequences removed and been reduced (or, if you prefer, raised) to the level of sheer appearances, where their meaning can be more powerfully articulated and more exactly perceived. (443)

Similarly, NASA, and specifically, the U.S. manned space flight program, was a way for Americans to talk to themselves about themselves. As Trento (1987) has show, neither the U.S. military nor the CIA had any interest in manned space flight. The meaning of the space flight program was symbolic from the outset and remained so. In the case of the space shuttle *Challenger,* as we shall see, the image that I had of the voyage—Americans transcending their differences and their finitude, floating blissfully together in space—was in fact the meaning of the voyage itself.

But when the meaning of social institutions is symbolic, does this not raise the possibility of a rift between the meaning of the symbol and the social reality it is presumed to reflect? And if so, does that not raise the possibility that a society may become so enamored of the image it creates of itself that the fact that it is only a symbol may be forgotten or repressed? And if that were to happen, could that not make a problem for the very existence of the symbol itself?

For, as Goffman has shown (1959), these commentaries, these works of art require a staging, and the staging is not, and cannot be, part of the work of art. If a society were to fall too much in love with what it was telling itself about itself, the staging of the performance might become impossible.

I propose that the symbol of manned space flight that NASA intended, and was intended to, project came to contradict the social and organizational realities that were necessary for its staging. Briefly put, the symbol of manned space flight had become a symbol of limitless, effortless perfection in which constraint appeared only as an illusion. But the organization of advanced technology cannot take place in an atmosphere of limitless, effortless perfection. It requires a self-critical sobriety in which the consciousness of limitation is ever present. Rather than experiencing constraint as an illusion, one must be fully conscious that illusion is a constraint. Under the circumstances it was inevitable that something would give way. It turned out to be the space shuttle itself.

NARCISSISM AND AMERICAN CULTURE

In earlier chapters, I have discussed the internal workings of NASA in terms of a theory about organizations as projects for the return to narcissism. In this chapter I would like to indulge a train of thought that was suggested to me by the commentator Daniel Schorr, who pointed out what tremendous pressure for perfection had been placed on NASA by the news media. This suggested that analyses concentrating solely on what was going within NASA miss the meaning of NASA itself, and particularly of NASA's manned space flight mission. Drawing the boundaries more widely I realized that NASA was serving a symbolic function within the overall American culture.

In effect, upon NASA had fallen the burden of maintaining the narcissism of a strikingly, and perhaps increasingly narcissistic American culture (Lasch 1979, 1984). Through NASA, Americans were telling themselves that, despite the drubbing the U.S. Army took in Vietnam, despite the fact that American industry could not compete within the American market, much less abroad, despite the fact that many American cities had become modern instantiations of Hobbes "state of nature"—despite all this, still America was perfect. This again is narcissism, but on the level of the whole society.

Gaining a sense of the place of narcissism in American society requires a concept that I have not made much use of before: the superego. In the normal case, partly through projection and partly through introjection, an individual comes to have a relatively stable image of the person he or she is "supposed to be" or "should be" in order again to become the center of a loving world. Thus, a set of obligations is understood as expressing the conditions for the attainment of the ego ideal. This set of obligations provides the basis for the superego.

The superego gives a sense of direction to one's life and especially to those areas of life, such as one's organizational role, that are dominated and motivated by a sense of the appropriate. But between people and within the same person at different times, the balance between the fantastical aspect of the ego ideal and its obligatory aspect, the superego, may differ. When the obligatory aspect gains the upper hand and displaces the fantastical, we speak of the person as an obsessive-compulsive. When the obligatory aspect is very weak as compared with the fantastical, we refer to the person as narcissistic. Such persons may be said to identify themselves with their own ego ideal.

The difference between the narcissistic and the normal case, then, has a developmental dimension. The obligatory component develops through the course of a person's life—a course that begins with primary narcissism but that progresses through identifications with adults whom the individual regards as having attained the ego ideal and whom the individual strives to become like. Thus, the normal person believes that he or she needs to live up to certain standards, to "become somebody" in order to attain the ego ideal. The narcissist, maintaining an infantile orientation to the world, believes that he or she is already the ego ideal and in one way or another denies those elements of reality that contradict this preferred vision.

One of the most deeply regressive forms of this denial is known in psychoanalytic theory as the denial of difference. As used by Freudians, the denial of difference refers to the infantile fantasy that the mother has a penis. Chasseguet-Smirgel (1985, 1986) points to the function that this serves in the preoedipal emotional life of the male child. It allows him to think of the mother as being sexually complete and not sexually requiring the father. In this fashion, the child can conceive maintaining its sense of unity with the mother, a sense that would not be disturbed by the child's recognition that its infantile sexuality will not suffice to keep the mother satisfied. Thus the denial of difference is a denial of sexual differentiation and at the same time something deeper—a denial of the difference between the generations, of children and adults. The child denies that it has to become like the father—that it has to become an adult—in order to have union with the mother. It does not have to do anything. It can have everything just by being what it is.

The denial of difference is the image that spoke to me out of the picture of the astronauts in their unisex flight suits: sexual dedifferentiation and generational dedifferentiation. Add to this the idea that ethnic dedifferentiation represents a denial of rivalry among siblings for exclusive union with the mother, and you have the whole photograph.

But at a deeper level, and one that will permit me to return to the proposition that the symbol of manned space flight had become inconsistent with the social reality that would have had to support it, note that the denial of difference is at the same time a denial of the difference between the world and the self, reality and fantasy, achievement and desire, between technology and magic. A society thinking of itself in these terms, living its emotional life on this level, would have lost the motivational basis for technological achievement.

THE DEGENERATION OF THE SYMBOL OF MANNED SPACE FLIGHT: THE SINGLE COMBAT WARRIOR

In evaluating the symbol of manned space flight presented in the case of the *Challenger,* it is useful to compare it to an earlier symbol of manned space flight, as described by Tom Wolfe in *The Right Stuff* (1979).

For Wolfe, the symbol called for by the American public, and happily generated by the original American astronauts, was the symbol of the "single combat warrior." By launching *Sputnik,* the first artificial satellite, the Russians threatened, in the words of Senate Majority Leader Lyndon Johnson, to seize "the high ground" (71) of space. America was in a panic. When the original astronauts were chosen, during a period in which American rockets did nothing but blow up, the adulation for them was instant. They, our bravest and best test pilots, would ride the rockets into space and symbolically do battle with the Russians, in much the same way that earlier lone warriors had stood for the armies of which they were part and prefigured or replaced the battle between the armies themselves. The public would grant them anything. It would be the loving world of which they were the center. It would fulfill for them the ego ideal.

But note that in this case there is no question of just being oneself. Attainment of the ego ideal here is contingent upon these astronauts *doing something.* And, indeed, doing something pretty impressive. Single combat with the Russians was not regarded as a merely mortal performance. On the contrary, the astronaut would take upon himself the role of a protecting god. He would stand against the hostile forces that surrounded the whole nation and vanquish them. At the deepest level, the astronaut would challenge the separation of self and the world that is the root cause of our anxiety and overcome it by overcoming the world. To be sure, as with Geertz's cockfight, nothing of the sort will have taken place. Nonetheless, the very real danger in which the astronauts are placed makes real such overcoming as they may achieve and at least gives a content to the fantasy. It gives the fantasy an active character.

We can see the active character of the ego ideal in the symbol of the astronauts more clearly by focusing upon the creation of the symbol from the other side—from the side of the astronauts. There, the symbol was a pilot with "the Right Stuff."

The idea of being seen as pilots, and not simply as passengers was the equivalent of requiring that they be seen as being in control, and not just passive participants ("Spam in a can"). It would turn the flight from a mere experience into an achievement. This aspect of the symbol was so important to the astronauts that when they realized how much power their iconic stature gave to them, they used that power to force the redesign of their vehicle from a "capsule" to a "spacecraft," by adding elements to it that would approximate as much as possible the control systems of an airplane. If they were to gain adulation, they would gain it by flying.

The idea of the "Right Stuff," as Wolfe describes it, contains the sort of mythic elements that only the ego ideal possesses. Wolfe likens it to the Presbyterian doctrine of being one of the elect.[1] It was not something that one could gain; one could only prove that one had it. And if one had it, as with Presbyterian grace, one neither had, nor need have, any fear of death. It is clearly a symbol of prevailing over death, of immortality—the ultimate in being the center of a loving world. Moreover, it is immortality that knows itself to be immortality. Analogous to the Presbyterian elect's certainty of election, to have the right stuff is to have courage without trying to have courage. The proof of the right stuff is perfect calmness in the face of what appears to be absolute catastrophe.

But if the primitive character of the wish is clear enough, what is equally clear, in terms of the manned flight program, is the demanding character of the proof that one had the right stuff. This proof was nothing short of being the perfect pilot. The death of a pilot meant that he did not have the right stuff. No excuses were allowed. The opposition right stuff/death was absolute—even tautological. As Wolfe put it: "There are no accidents and no fatal flaws in the machines: there are only pilots with the wrong stuff" (34). Moreover, the attitude behind perfection in piloting could not be one of complacency. Absolute mastery of detail was required. This is not to deny self-confidence. On the contrary, self-confidence was part of having the right stuff. But in the same fashion, so was an obsessive concentration on detail. Both were expressions of the right stuff. Taken together, the emotional control in the attainment of perfect sangfroid and the perfection in the process of flying itself added to a list of "shoulds" and "supposed tos" that was, perhaps, demanding beyond what human beings could sustain. These people intended to be the center of a loving world, but they did not think of attaining this position as an effortless achievement. It was precisely in those terms that they demanded to be accepted and in which they crafted, consciously and unconsciously, the symbol of themselves and, by extension, of the U.S. manned space flight program.

In comparing the symbol of the original astronauts with that of the astronauts of 51-L, I should like to consider Robert T. Hohler's journalistic account (1986) of the process of symbol construction. In this case, what was clearly the most symbolic aspect of the program, the so-called "Teacher in Space" program was recorded with a focus on Christa McAuliffe, who was eventually chosen to be the first "teacher in space" and was exclusively covered by Hohler.

THE DEGENERATION OF THE SYMBOL OF MANNED
SPACE FLIGHT: THE DENIAL OF DIFFERENCE
AND DISNEYLAND IN SPACE

The manned space flight program was symbolic in intent right from the beginning. But as we have seen, the original symbol was one of the astronauts prevailing over death through competence. The contrast with the symbol constructed of the *Challenger* astronauts could not be more striking. Not only does death disappear in this symbol, but competence does as well. For competence in overcoming death has become unnecessary. In developmental terms, the symbol presented here has its home in mental life before the concept of death has yet developed. But if the concept of overcoming death through competence has become unnecessary, it has also become impossible. It has become undefined, meaningless. And the result is that it became motivationally impossible. The fact that death itself followed from this regression cannot be surprising. In an enterprise as dangerous as the space shuttle's, it became inevitable. All of these are aspects of the denial of difference.

Consider the picture of the smiling astronauts. Recall the way this made my imagination soar: "Look what America has done! America has transcended its cleavages, men and women fly together, the races fly together, the ages fly together. Even the children can fly." I said before that this fantasy was not my own construct, but was the result of a carefully crafted symbol. Consider Hohler's account of the shuttle:

Its passengers would include Francis Scobee, Judith Resnik, Elisson Onizuka and Ronald McNair, four of the thirty-five astronauts who were selected from a crush of more than eight thousand applicants in January 1978. They were a military pilot, a Jewish woman, an Asian American and a black—*symbols of NASA's commitment to carry America's cultural rainbow toward the stars.* (46, emphasis added)

And this about McAuliffe:

On cue, she talked about looking down from the shuttle on "Spaceship Earth" —a Disney concept—imagining a planet where no differences divided blacks and whites, Arabs and Jews, Russians and Americans.
"It's going to be wonderful to see us as one people, a world with no boundaries," she said. "I can't wait to bring back that humanistic spirit." (15)

What is striking to me about these images is not only the denial of social differentiation that they represent, but the way they manifest the denial of difference in their failure to distinguish the symbol from reality. Christa McAuliffe will go into space and "see us as one people" with no differences between blacks and whites, rich and poor, and so forth. But of course there are differences, and flying a hundred miles above them does not reconcile those differences; it only obscures them.

Or consider the idea of sending America's "cultural rainbow" toward the stars. At a time when America's racial groups appear to be becoming irretrievably divided, when America's sexual relationships have become so problematic that a recent writer has spoken of our youth as "the unromantic generation," when heavily armed neo-Nazi sects are trying to organize the secession of the American Northwest, the idea of America's cultural rainbow as being a unity in diversity is simply absurd and the idea of bringing it into being by flying people in space is bizarre. Indeed, from a psychoanalytic point of view it is precisely the tensions among these groups that makes the symbol of their resolution attractive. What gives this image its clinical cast is the failure to distinguish between symbol and reality.

Returning to Geertz's analysis of the cockfight, recall his observation that the cockfight, stripped of consequences, could become a form of art. The same can be said of the space shuttle phenomenon. But it is worthwhile to note that the Balinese did not think that the separation of the cockfight from the surrounding social reality constituted a *replacement* of that reality. In the case of American culture, the symbol appeared to represent precisely that. Indeed, the backdrop for this play of the imagination in space would seem to be the idea that distance can establish the imaginary realm as an alternative reality that has as much claim on the psyche as the world in which we live. This is the denial of difference in a particularly acute form.

The denial of social differentiation is an aspect of the denial of difference that puts the sense of reality into a precarious position. But at least as a fantasy it gives a positive sense of direction to the process and a content that is relatively harmless. Much more insidious are those aspects of the denial of difference that directly undermine the possibility of competence. The selection of Christa McAuliffe as the teacher in space provides a case study of how this happened.

If the sense of competence were to be reinforced, and if Americans were telling themselves something about the necessity of being able to do something in order to participate in utopia and fulfill their ego ideal, the selection of the astronauts would have been made on the basis of a perceived difference, an achieved difference, between the astronaut and the ordinary person. But as Hohler makes plain, the selection of McAuliffe was intended to give precisely the opposite message. Thus, whatever the wisdom or lack of wisdom of the teacher in space program itself, many of the other finalists had considerable accomplishments to their credit. McAuliffe had none. McAuliffe was selected, I propose, because she was just like everybody else and because she was proud of it:

Christa was not the brightest of the ten finalists. One of them was a prize-winning playwright and poet, and another had been invited by the French government to study language, literature and culture there for a year. Most of them had graduated from schools more prestigious than Christa's alma mater of Framingham State College. One had even graduated Phi Beta Kappa from Stanford University.

On paper, some of them seemed to push Christa to the back of the class. There was a former fighter pilot, a film producer and a woman who, among other adventures, had climbed the Andes and Himalayas and crossed the Atlantic in a thirty-one foot sailboat. Several of them knew much more about space and science than Christa knew, and the projects most of them had proposed for the six-day journey made Christa's idea of keeping a diary look rather ordinary.

Which of course was the difference. Christa was the girl next door, and more. No other finalist matched her potential for getting NASA's message across. (10, emphasis added)

What was the message, and why could she get it across so well?

She was even a Girl Scout. Who better to sell the wonders of space than a woman who once sold more Girl Scout cookies than anyone in her neighborhood? And she still had the touch. She was bold, charming and convincing, and when she said in her teacher's voice "I want to prove that space is for everyone," people believed her. (6)

She told Lathlaen [another teacher in space finalist] she had done her best to convince NASA that she could "humanize the technology of the space age" by showing the world that "there are real people up there." (6)

When a reporter asked her why she wanted to go into space . . . she talked about her journal, about how her perspective as an ordinary person would "demistify" the space program and about her vision of the world as a global village, of one people living together. (106)

With a push from NASA, the media had stumbled upon a new concept: the teacher as hero. . . . Through it all, Christa was one of us. (180)

Her selection, in other words, expressed the message that the American public did not have to do anything to experience utopia in space, but that they could do it just as they were. Americans were telling themselves through the medium of McAuliffe that they did not have to do anything in order to attain the ego ideal, to be perfect—they already were perfect, and it was only their temporary boundedness to the world that caused their anxiety. Spaceflight was seen as simply the realization of that perfection. The meaning of Christa McAuliffe's selection, I submit, was the expression of American narcissism. Her primary task would be its legitimation.

Thus, if I am correct, the selection of Christa McAuliffe as the teacher in space represented a critical aspect of the denial of difference. It represented the denial of the difference between the generations—of the fact that one has to learn to do something, to attain competence, in order to attain perfection.

But showing how the regressive character of the ego ideal in its most acute form is exemplified by McAuliffe's selection requires that one more observation be made. What needs to be finally understood is that the image of the shuttle was intended to appeal to children and at the same time to the child in each of us. In this respect we cannot forget that there are virtually myriads of ordinary occupations. The choice of the teacher from among these needs further explanation. Each of us has had teachers, and children have teachers still. Thus, a teacher can be seen as a universal type. But the universality of the symbolism of the teacher is based upon the universality of childhood. Christa McAuliffe would come back from space, and then her job would be to spread the news. But she would spread the news to children and to the child in each of us. McAuliffe's mission was to put the symbolism of spaceflight into a perspective that made sense within the cognitive orientation of the child.

McAuliffe's thought concerning Barbara Morgan, who was to be McAuliffe's backup, evinces her attitude on the place of children in space clearly enough:

She arrived at the space center with a camera dangling from her neck, her eyes aglitter and her dark-brown, shoulder-length hair pulled back on one side with a clip. She looked like a child on her first day at Disneyland, Christa thought. She looked like she belonged on the shuttle. (98)

Thus, NASA had chosen to cast its ideal as a child's ideal. Ultimately, it seems to me, this transformation in its image most closely represented the rift between NASA's image of itself and the reality that it required. For there is no place in the child's world for the sort of painstaking care that spaceflight requires. In a word, the child's view of the world does not recognize technology; it dwells on magic. Understanding itself within the child's point of view, NASA's image of itself became incompatible with its technological necessities. I shall return to this shortly, but first it will be useful to consider the transformation of symbols of manned spaceflight from that of single combat warfare to that of Disneyland in space.

THE SUCCESSION OF SYMBOLS

If the symbolic function of spaceflight had changed from test pilot competence to ordinary American mediocrity, a clash between these symbols might be expected. Surely the test pilots would not let the dramatization of their ego ideal be overcome without a struggle. In fact, there is evidence of such a struggle, but it appears to have been rather feeble. Hohler describes McAuliffe's encounter with Dick Scobee, the mission commander, thus:

Scobee had worried her. She knew her meteoric flash across the media sky had bred contempt among a few people in the space agency. She knew her promise to "humanize" space travel had not sat well with astronauts who also claimed to be human. And she knew she was an outsider who had been thrust into one of the world's most exclusive clubs without a vote by its members. Little had frightened her more than the crew rejecting her as a public relations ornament. . . . She wondered most about Scobee.

At first glance, she thought, he seemed like the astronauts of her youth, wholesome and handsome, tall, blue-eyed and ruggedly built with a square jaw and an air of self-confidence. And right from the start Scobee left no doubt that he was in charge, that Christa was a member of a team that had been chosen for a space mission, not a joy ride.

"Those are no firecrackers they'll be lighting under our tails," he told her. "Those things are for real."

But soon he eased up, and Christa realized he was not the macho jet jockey she had feared. He was much like her, an ordinary person who had accomplished the extraordinary, the first enlisted man to rise through the ranks to the astronaut corps. (149)

And it appears from Hohler's account that Scobee would not have disagreed with this unheroic assessment:

When he returned from his first shuttle mission in 1984, he told the students at his former high school, "If I can do it, anybody can."

Scobee had come to NASA headquarters to review the preliminary plans for Christa's shuttle lessons. He talked with her for a while and began to see a little of himself in her, a person of modest background *and modest talents* who had maintained her humility in the face of extraordinary success. (149–50, emphasis added)

To understand the full significance of these judgments, it is useful to consider what "extraordinary accomplishment" and "extraordinary success" mean here. Remember in this regard that Christa McAuliffe had not done anything yet and that, indeed, given that there was to be nothing requiring competence in the task she was to undertake in space, she would not do anything later. The conclusion must be that the accomplishment consisted in being selected itself. Thus, the traditional formulation in which adulation arises from achievement has been short-circuited: adulation *is* the achievement. One need not do anything to be somebody.

This is a point that calls for some elaboration. In earlier discussion we saw that in the normal case, the individual is connected to the fulfillment of the ego ideal through the superego. An obligation, a deed, stands between the separate individual and the individual as center of a loving world. But in the case of McAuliffe, the instrumental deed seems to have become superfluous. McAuliffe experienced herself as already the center of a loving world, and her selection merely confirmed this predestined appointment. It does not go too far to suggest that McAuliffe experienced the connection between herself, as she was, and the world that loved her as essential. She could call forth the loving response of others just by being herself. She was their meaning, indeed their very cause. Hence, she could take pride in the fact that she was selected by others and see this selection as her own accomplishment, even despite the fact that she knew that she had done nothing to earn it. Here again is the denial of difference, this time in the form of the denial of the difference between the self and others. In such a fashion the celebrity replaces the hero, and competence is overcome.

But sad to say, symbols of competence had been losing their significance for some time. Wolfe describes part of this process:

The prestige of the Astronaut absolutely dominated flying, and the Air Force was determined to be the prime supplier of that breed . . . .

To tell the truth, the brass had gone slightly bananas over this business of producing astronauts. They had even set up a "charm school" in Washington for the leading candidates. The best of the young pilots . . . flew to Washington and were given a course in how to impress the NASA selection panels in Houston. And it was dead serious! They listened to pep talks by Air Force generals. . . . They went through drills on how to talk on their feet—and that was the more sensible, credible part of the course. From there it got right down to the level of cotillion etiquette. They were told what to wear to the interviews with the engineers and astronauts. . . . They were told what to drink at the social get-togethers in Houston. . . . They were told how to put their hands on their hips (if they must) . . .

And the men went through it all willingly! Without a snigger! The brass's passion for the astronaut business was nothing compared to that of the young pilots themselves. Edwards [Air Force Base, the Air Force test facility] had always been the precise location on the map of the apex of the pyramid of the right stuff itself. And now it was just another step on the way up. . . .

The glamor of the space program was such that there was no longer any arguing against it. In addition to the chances for honor, glory, fame and the celebrity treatment, all the new hot dogs could see something else . . . the Astronaut Life . . . The *Life* contract . . . $25,000 a year over and above your salary . . . veritable *mansions* in the suburbs . . . free Corvettes . . . and the tastiest young cookies [i.e., girls] imaginable. . . . The vision of all the little sugarplums danced above the mighty ziggurat [i.e., the test pilot's ascent to his ego ideal] . . . and all these young hot dogs looked upon it like people who believed in miracles. (413)

Thus, over a period of time, the astronauts themselves had abandoned their own ego ideal of competence in the overcoming of death. They had moved from an ego ideal they could conceive of creating through their own actions, of realizing themselves in, to the ego ideal of the organizational man—an ego ideal created outside of themselves, fitting someone else, and which they could approximate only through acts of subservience. Competence in the face of death had become, not the condition for their ego ideal, but simply a selection criterion among many others in the pursuit of an ego ideal whose content had become the simple consumption of commodities. They had, indeed, become just like everybody else.

FROM RELIGION TO ANIMISM

In his classic study on the origins of religion, *Totem and Taboo* (1938), Freud differentiated among three "systems of thought": the animistic (mythological), the religious, and the scientific, which he found in both the historical and the individual developmental orders. Among the characteristics differentiating these stages is variation in the attitude toward what he calls the omnipotence of thought:

In the animistic stage man ascribes omnipotence to himself; in the religious phase he has ceded it to the gods, but without seriously giving it up, for he reserves to himself the right to control the gods by influencing them in some way or other in the interests of his wishes. In the scientific attitude towards life there is no longer any room for man's omnipotence; he has acknowledged his smallness and has submitted to death as to all other natural necessities in a spirit of resignation. (875)

In this differentiation it seems clear enough that the "single combat warrior" view of manned spaceflight belonged to the religious stage of development. Here, the astronauts were seen as gods who could protect the people and upon whom the people could depend, or at least upon whom they could depend if the gods were kept in the proper frame of mind. Significantly, Freud locates the religious phase in the developmental period of dependence on the parents. Thus, from this perspective, the shift of symbolism from "single combat warrior" to "Disneyland in space" can be seen as a regressive shift from the religious phase to the animistic.

A key element in Freud's analysis of animism is magic. I have argued that when the concept of spaceflight was cast in the child's perspective, the concept of technology was lost and replaced by the concept of magic. On magic, Freud quotes J. G. Frazer: "'men mistook the order of their ideas for the order of nature, and hence imagined that the control which they have, or seem to have, over their thoughts, permitted them to have a corresponding control over things'" (871). He adds that the instrumental factor, the factor that leads primitives to believe that they can accomplish things through magic, is evidently the power of the wish: "We need only assume that primitive man had great confidence in the power of his wishes" (872). Thus, the primitive feels that by representing the fulfilled wish, a state comparable to the child's play, he has brought it about. Moreover:

If play and imitative representation suffice for the child and for primitive man, it must not be taken as a sign of modesty, in our sense, or of resignation due to the realization of their impotence; on the contrary, it is the very obvious result of the excessive valuation of their wish, of the will that depends upon the wish and of the paths the wish takes.

And then Freud adds: "In time the psychic accent is displaced from the motives of the magic act to its means, namely to the act itself" (872).

Again, Freud directly equates the animistic phase with narcissism, in the sense that the overvaluation of psychic acts that give rise to magic accounts for "the unshaken confidence in the capacity to dominate the world and the inaccessibility to the obvious facts which would enlighten man as to his real place in the world" (876).

Thus, it is the narcissism of the animistic phase that makes magic seem natural and makes science impossible within it:

Animism, the first conception of the world which man succeeded in evolving, was therefore psychological. It did not yet require any science to establish it, for science sets in only after we have realized that we do not know the world and that we must therefore seek means of getting to know it. (877)

Finally, Freud notes:

Only in one field has the omnipotence of thought been retained in our own civilization, namely in art. In art alone it still happens that man, consumed by his wishes, produces something similar to the gratification of these wishes, and this playing, thanks to artistic illusion, calls forth effects as if it were something real. (877)

Here we have the original terms of this inquiry, in which I compared the U.S. manned spaceflight program with Geertz's Balinese cockfight, seeing them as art forms. I asked what would happen if a symbol that had become incompatible with the social reality necessary for its staging were actually adopted to replace the reality?

CONSEQUENCES OF THE DEGENERATION OF THE SYMBOL

Looking at the transformation in the image of manned spaceflight, from single combat warfare to Disneyland in space, and seeing it as representative of a deeper shift from the religious to the animistic system of thought gives ample material in terms of which to consider the loss of technological capacity that gave rise to the space shuttle catastrophe.

Consider the astronauts as single combat warriors, seen by others as gods, and seeing themselves as bearers of the right stuff that will enable them to prevail over death through competence. There is no conflict here between the message and its staging, the symbol and the technology that makes it possible. On the contrary, the astronauts, knowing that the technology must work perfectly if they are to survive must have obsessive concern with just that technological perfection. This is an aspect of their competence. Moreover, with regard to others who are involved in the technological process, that obsessive concern must manifest itself as a deep motivational thrust. For while it perhaps goes too far to say that NASA and other aerospace workers felt that they had to protect the single combat warriors, they certainly felt themselves as having a stake in the warriors' victory. They knew very well that the mission was dangerous and that victory was not assured but required their best efforts if it was to be attained. Moreover, the astronauts' role as god/parent/protector gave them authority. These were gods that had to be loved, honored, and obeyed if they were to protect. Competent work on the part of the aerospace workers would constitute this love, honor, and obedience.

Thus, Wolfe tells this story concerning Gus Grissom, one of the original astronauts:

Gus Grissom was out in San Diego in the Convair plant, where they were working on the Atlas rocket . . . and then the astronauts [were] supposed to say a few words, and all at once Gus realizes it's his turn to say something, and he is petrified. He opens his mouth and out come the words: "Well . . . do good work!" It's an ironic remark, implying: ". . . because its my ass that'll be sitting on your freaking rocket." But the workers started cheering like mad. They started cheering as if they had just heard the most moving and inspiring message of their lives: *Do good work!* After all, it's little Gus's ass on top of our rocket! They stood there for an eternity and cheered their brains out while Gus gazed blankly upon them. . . . Not only that, the workers—not the management, but the workers!—had a flag company make up a huge banner, and they strung it up high in the main work bay, and it said: DO GOOD WORK. (147–48)

How can anything like this take place with regard to Disneyland in space? In the narcissistic world in which NASA had come to live, there was no death. There was not even any danger. Certainly there was no more danger than one would find on a good roller-coaster ride—existing for the purpose of exhilaration. Moreover, perfect workers could not make mistakes. Indeed, there was not even any necessity to pay attention. After all, if the ritual forms were followed, the magic would assuredly take place. Wishing would make it so. The symbol had become incompatible with the possibility of its staging and had been chosen over it.

In referring to the power that the primitive and the child place in magic, I am going back to what I have already said about the denial of difference. Here again is the failure to distinguish reality from fantasy that led people to believe that if they could send a harmonious social mixture into orbit around the world they could create social harmony. In this connection, the space shuttle itself became a magical instrument, akin to a magician's wand. Its purpose was to transform the wish into the reality, and it did not need to be fussed over in order to be able to do that. To be sure, the space ship had had to prove its efficacy, but it had already done so during the early days of spaceflight when it took men to the moon. Having proved its capacity to create magical transformations, the space shuttle had nothing left to show.

This is the context in which the sorts of abuses of organizational process described earlier occurred at NASA: appointments to technical position based purely on politics, loss of technical capacity to properly oversee contractors, submission of schedules that could not be met, commitment to projects that were grossly underfunded, extreme miscalculation of risks, suppression of unpleasant information, degeneration of organizational processes into empty rituals, and so on.

In a word, I submit that what occurred was a neurotic regression of the symbolic structure in which the American people saw manned spaceflight and through it themselves. This regression went from a religious framework, where danger was acknowledged, possibility of failure was present, and competence was required, to an animistic system, in which safety was assured, perfection was assumed, and nothing was required at all. In the first system, technological achievement was possible. In the second it was not.

REGRESSION IN ORGANIZATIONAL CULTURE

If indeed a regression has occurred in the symbol of manned space flight and if this regression is part of a larger shift in American culture, then evidence of this regression should appear in other cultural areas, such as organizational culture.

In an article that began as the 1981 presidential address to the American Academy of Management, Cummings (1983) described the rise of what he called *management by ideology,* which, he said, was supplanting what he called *management by information.*

The two types of management differ in a number of ways, according to Cummings, the most important of which for the present purposes is this:

Management by information encourages participants to engage in hypothesis *testing* about aspects of their organizational existence: to query, to question, to ask, to explore, and, most of all, to learn. Management by ideology as a logic encourages a participant to accept hypothesis *confirmation* and *affirmation:* to accept, to believe, to commit, to expound accepted doctrine, and even to glorify, and never to question, except in private, sanctioned arenas and audiences. (533)

It seems clear enough that the shift from management by information to management by ideology represents a shift from an orientation toward reality to an orientation toward fantasy—it involves the loss of the superego. As such, it appears to manifest the same regression we have seen in the image of manned space flight.

Furthermore, the timing of Cummings's observation suggests that he is referring to the same transformation in organizational culture that has seen the rise of symbolic management as an important focus of organizational change, supplanting, at least in part, earlier organizational change strategies, such as job enrichment.

Organizational change strategies tend to invoke what I refer to above as the "organization ideal." As I noted in chapter 2, the organization ideal, which represents utopia in the form of an organization, is represented in traditional theories of organizational change by notions such as self-actualization (Argyris 1957). Such notions imply that at the peak of individual and organizational development, there can be a unity of individual happiness and spontaneity, on the one hand, and maximal performance and productivity, on the other. In current theories of cultural management the organization ideal is represented by such ideas as the "excellent organization" (Peters and Waterman 1982) and the "strong culture" organization (Deal and Kennedy 1982). But notice that there is a difference between the traditional and current theories.

In the traditional theories the idea of the organizational participant as resident in utopia is clear enough. Thus, for example, Hackman, Olson, Janson, and Purdy (1975) liken working at an enriched job to playing golf. But even if the utopian element is a fantasy, it is at least conceived as a fantasy in which one can participate only by doing something. Entry into the utopia represented by the symbolically managed excellent organization, by contrast, is conceived of as being only a matter of participating in the organization's culture—that is to say, of believing and valuing certain things. Thus, as with the regression from "the single combat warrior" to "Disneyland in space," the necessity for satisfying the demands of the superego, the obligation to do something as a requirement for participation in utopia has become lost.

CONCLUSION: AGAINST THE MANIC DEFENSE

In attempting to understand the shift from management by information to management by ideology, Cummings (1983) offers the following explanation:

Now there is a reemergence of management by ideology because of turbulence in environments, because of rapidity of change, because of the increased sophistication of the receiver of facts, and . . . because distortion and intentional untruths are a common, daily fare for many organizational participants. (533)

And he adds: "Without this return to management by ideology, the only alternative would be alienation, resentment, and despair" (533).

There is no need to dwell overly long on the context for Cummings's remarks. The United States, which in 1945 truly was the center of a loving world, has lost both that centrality and that love. What Cummings observes is the fact that American organizations have not responded at all well to this loss.

This loss has brought out problems that were always there, but that were never thought to matter very much. Within the context of American narcissism, these problems have come to seem insurmountable. Rather than giving up the narcissism and attempting to grapple realistically with these problems, we have given up realism and reinforced our narcissism. Thus, what we see here is a further development of what I referred to in chapter 2 as the manic defense—and this time on the level of the whole society.

8

Conclusion: Addiction and Recovery

In bringing this project to a close, it may be worthwhile to first observe that there is nothing in psychoanalytic theory, history, or logic that necessitates a happy ending for the account of decay that I have presented here. On the contrary, history especially suggests that the trajectory that takes social systems from triumph to *hubris* and then to decay is a common one. Thus, Lord Byron from *Childe Harold:*

> There is the moral of all human tales:
> 'Tis but the same rehearsal of the past,
> First Freedom, and then Glory—when that fails,
> Wealth, vice, corruption—barbarianism at last.

Nonetheless, while the human capacities for vanity and self-deception, which of course bring such stories to their sad end, are moral facts that are easy to observe, so it is also true that the human capacities for honesty and growth are also facts. And if, in the course of history, it has been true that the positive side of the human moral balance has come up wanting, so it is also true that there has never been a time when human moral courage was more requisite for human survival and when, I suspect, even if unconsciously, it has been known to be so requisite.

CULTURAL MANAGEMENT AS A CORRECTIVE FOR DECADENCE

The condition of generalized and systemic ineffectiveness which I have attributed to the advancement of narcissistic process, whether or not one wishes to explain it in these terms, is clear enough in American industry and is even clear *to* American industry. As is their way, having perceived a problem, Americans have called for an instant answer (McGill 1988). They have not had a great deal of difficulty in finding individuals who have been ready and willing to sell them one. The dominant voices here belong to those (Peters and Waterman 1982; Deal and Kennedy 1982) who propose to deal with America's organizational problems through cultural or symbolic management.

This school of thought provides an intellectual expression of the regression we saw in chapter 7 as well as of the totalitarian impulse we have considered throughout this work. Following Weick's (1977) claim that "reality is a metaphor" that is "enacted" rather than discovered,[1] it asserts that management can control "reality," such as it is, by controlling the collective mind of the organization's participants—the organization's culture.[2] What we can understand on the basis of the previous discussion is that this idea about the efficacy of management is just another expression of the self-idealization and the narcissistic loss of reality that are themselves central dynamics at the root of the cultural problem that American industry manifests.

The appeal of this sort of thing to troubled American management is understandable. It enables them to conceive of regaining centrality in a loving world without acknowledging that it has been their *hubris* that has made them powerless in a world turned hostile. Moreover, successful or not, they can maintain their self-idealization: If the organization comes again to prosper, it is because the management changed its culture; if it does not, it is because the employees were obstinate in maintaining their bad attitudes. Nonetheless, within the context of what has been said, it seems clear enough that this form of cultural management is only organizational totalitarianism become systematic and conscious. To the extent that it was organizational totalitarianism that was the cause of American organizational decadence, it seems unlikely that a distilled form of it is going to be effective as a cure.

Having said that, however, I think it is time to note that a good deal of what the theorists of cultural management say is quite correct. More than correct, it is obvious. Thus, Peters and Waterman (1982) emphasize the value excellent companies place on quality and service, their staying close to the customer, paying attention to the people who do the work, giving people the autonomy they need to do their work, and so on. In other words, these organizations highly value and support *the process of work itself.* Indeed, this is a point with which Peters and Waterman would agree. They say, for example: "the excellent companies were brilliant on the basics" (13). And they say that it is this quality of placing importance on those basic matters that directly support the work process that differentiates the excellent companies from those that are mediocre.

It seems to me, however, that the foregoing analysis gives a different slant to Peters and Waterman's observations. Instead of asking how organizations can recreate the culture that generates excellence, we need to ask how it is, since that culture simply consists in the positive valuation of work, that it got lost? How is it possible, in other words, that work organizations ceased valuing work? Indeed, it appears that there is something about the culture of the work organizations these theorists criticize that seems to impede the work process. How did that happen?[3] Answering this question requires that we proceed through analysis of another phenomenon, also thought to represent a narcissistic disorder (Kernberg 1975)—addiction generally and alcoholism specifically.

ALCOHOLISM AND ORGANIZATIONAL DECAY

To say that alcoholism is a narcissistic disorder suggests that the function of drinking, for the alcoholic, is to use the chemical ethyl alcohol as a way of weakening the superego, deadening the pull of reality against his or her narcissistic fantasies, and thereby allowing those fantasies free reign. Thus, for the alcoholic, drinking is a way to induce a manic defense. Within this analysis, one has become an alcoholic when the self-centered world as seen within the intoxicated state is taken as one's real world. Hence, one needs to drink in order to resume contact with and verify one's own reality. It follows from this that, as one comes to take one's narcissistic fantasies as reality, the more out of touch with the real world one becomes, hence the more one needs to drink in order to "verify" one's fantasies, and, again, the further out of touch one becomes. Within this logic we can see the progressive element of the alcoholic's disease.

If this is so, it enables us to draw a parallel between alcoholism, on one hand, and the orientation taken toward the organization in organizational totalitarianism and decay, which as we have seen, also involves the manic defense.[4] Here, it is the fantasy of the organization ideal that is taken as the bedrock of reality. The fact that the organization is not the organization ideal may be explained by one's own imperfect identification with the organization. As we know, this is thought to be curable by deeper immersion in the organization fantasy, and especially by rising in the hierarchy.

Thus, the struggle for status becomes compulsive in much the same way as the alcoholic's drinking. As we have seen, the higher one's organizational status, the more acute is the difference between the isolation of one's existence and the centrality in a loving world that one is supposed to experience. And this reinforces the tendency for those who gain power within the organization to use that power to enforce the dramatization of their own perfection and the perfection of the organization. In this way, reality is pushed farther and farther away, which calls for more and more radical steps to be taken to preserve the dramatization of the organization ideal, such as the adoption of a conscious strategy of "cultural management." Thus, the progressive character of organizational totalitarianism and decay proceed according to the same logic as the progressive disease of alcoholism.

It is clear enough, then, why the positive valuation of work tends to fall away before the force of the organization's self-idealization. Work, after all, brings us into contact with reality (Freud 1961), and the organization's mythology is directed against reality. Work forces us to see and recognize our limitations. It makes us see that there is only so much that we can do. It requires us to understand that doing something well requires effort. It imposes upon us the fact that we are dependent on others who are outside of our control. None of these has any place in the organization fantasy. Dramatizing that fantasy, therefore, must impede the process of work and demean its importance. The organization ideal, like the alcoholic's drinking, is a denial. And it is exactly the facts that the process of work calls to our attention that the organization ideal arises to deny. Alcoholics, in this analysis, are not likely to quit drinking because it leads to the denial of reality. The denial of reality is the *reason why they drink.*

If the parallel between alcoholism and organizational totalitarianism and decay is correct, it suggests that there may be utility in pursuing an approach to the treatment of organizational decay through consideration of the method employed by an organization widely accepted as being successful in that area—Alcoholics Anonymous. In what follows I offer some preliminary and tentative observations from a study I have been conducting of that organization.

ALCOHOLICS ANONYMOUS AND THE RECOVERY
FROM NARCISSISM

The idea of alcoholism as a narcissistic disorder accords with ways that AAs characterize alcoholism both within the AA literature and as recurrent themes in the stories that AAs tell in meetings. For AAs, alcoholism is a "disease" on three levels: physical, mental, and spiritual. On the mental level the disease is characterized by grandiosity, self-centeredness, the need for control, the feeling of being someone special (i.e. "terminally unique"), the feeling that one should be judged by one's intentions rather than one's actions, and so on. What this adds up to is the belief that the world should revolve around oneself, taking one in the best possible light. Those who do not do this are experienced as violating some kind of law of nature, as being "bad" people against whom one is justified in holding grievances and resentments. The narcissistic trend here seems to me clear enough, even though AAs do not typically use the term.

More important for our purposes is the fact that the AA program seems directed against narcissism and aimed at the development of a viable way of life without narcissism, or at least without its pathological aspects. In what follows I wish to offer an absolutely minimalist explanation as to how the Alcoholics Anonymous program brings this about.

(1) The first step—Hitting bottom. The first step of the AA program says: "We admitted we were powerless over alcohol—that our lives had become unmanageable." The readiness to make this admission arises from what AA calls "hitting bottom."

AA members regard this as the doorway into the program. It is what makes the program possible and keeps it possible. For, in fact, the consciousness of oneself as an alcoholic needs to be maintained at all times for the rest of one's life. As AA says, once one has become an alcoholic, one remains an alcoholic until one dies.

AA members believe this most directly with regard to the physical aspects of the "disease" of alcoholism. They believe that alcoholics must abandon the idea of ever being social drinkers again, because any amount of drinking will lead alcoholics back to their former level of indulgence within a brief period of time. For our purposes, however, it is perhaps more important to see what this admission does on the mental level to the claims of narcissistic grandiosity.

What we see here is a very powerful and profound recognition of one's limitations. To the nonalcoholic, the degree of limitation expressed in the fact that one cannot ever drink alcohol again may not seem severe. For the alcoholic, however, it is a profound limitation indeed. By defining themselves as alcoholics, which is after all what got them into Alcoholics Anonymous, AA members place this sense of their own limitation right at the center of their identity. It does not go too far to say, then, that even over and above the abandonment of the grandiosity inherent in the intoxication experience itself, the acceptance of oneself as an alcoholic, and the admission of one's powerlessness over alcohol, focuses the direction of one's life directly against one's own tendencies toward grandiosity.

(2) Spirituality and mutuality. If the AA program offered only the rejection of one's narcissism, it would not be very appealing. What AAs see as the positive offering of the AA program is what they call "spirituality," which is introduced in the second and third steps of the program: (2) "Came to believe that a Power greater than ourselves could restore us to sanity;" and (3) "Made a decision to turn our will and our lives over to the care of God as we understood Him."

It is important to note, in understanding these steps, that AAs differentiate strongly between spirituality and religion.[5] Religion is what they learned as children. Typically, they have little good to say about it. On the contrary, they see it as part of the punitive world from which they were trying to escape through drinking. Indeed, my observation has been that it is the reluctance to have anything to do with anything that smacks of religion that is the greatest stumbling block in the AA's progress through the program and indeed is a hurdle that many potential Alcoholics Anonymous members simply cannot overcome.

That is perhaps why the second and third steps are so carefully worded to avoid calling upon the beginning AA member for more commitment than he or she is likely to be able to give at this point. Thus, step 2 says "could" restore us to sanity, permitting the AA to hedge with "if one existed." And step three says "Made a decision to turn our will and our lives over . . ." rather than "turned" them over. Finally, of course, there is the proviso that the God to whom one decides to turn things over is God "as we understood Him."

At any rate, AAs see the function of the second and third steps as that of opening the mind. They believe that if one opens one's mind to the possibility of spiritual experience, spiritual experience will come along to fill it. They offer testimony from their own cases that this happened to them. If their testimony is to be believed, their developing belief in their Higher Power is the direct result of felt spiritual experience, and is not simply an abstract and disembodied belief in anything. And indeed the change from the uniform skepticism of beginning AA members provides evidence that something profound must have happened.

It has been my observation that in most cases the new AA member accepts the Alcoholics Anonymous group itself as his or her Higher Power. To some extent, it seems to me, this remains the case for AA members generally. Thus, AA members agree that regular attendance at meetings and participation in the AA group remain essential for continued spiritual growth, no matter how long the AA has been sober. "God speaks through the people around the tables of AA" is a frequently heard expression of this view. How the AA group works in this way and what the AA experience of spirituality means generally are suggested by Ernest Kurtz (1979).

For Kurtz, the first critical insight that the Alcoholics Anonymous member needs, and which is represented in the first step, is that he or she is not God. The second critical insight is that he or she is not-God, which is to say that he or she shares an identity with others who are not God and who recognize themselves as such. It is this experience of shared identity, *in felt contrast with the essential loneliness and isolation of the alcoholic,* that is experienced as being a power greater than the self. Thus, for Kurtz, the acceptance of one's own limitation leads, in paradoxical fashion, to a strengthening mutual bond with others who are also limited. And this leads, again paradoxically, to an enrichment of the self that a denial of limitation could not provide.

Kurtz puts the matter this way:

The insight that weakness necessarily precedes strength and strength arises precisely out of weakness can check [the] spiral of insatiability. The acknowledgement of essential need to receive from others does not lead within Alcoholics Anonymous to infinitely increasing need to receive, but rather begets the ability to give. Acknowledging and accepting need removes the coercive power and insatiability that need imposes when denied. The recognition and acceptance of *both* self and others as not-God, and so mutually needful, mitigates imposition and demand. Awareness of this *mutuality* of needing others gives rise to a special kind of dialectic that sets limits to *both* the conviction that self is limited *and* the awareness of others as limited. The shared, honest acceptance that limitation, and specifically vulnerability to self-centeredness, is mutual, limits the very sense of vulnerability—the limitation of self-centeredness—from which it arises: this is the heart of the fellowship of Alcoholics Anonymous. (224)

Thus, to put the matter into psychoanalytic terms, the profound acceptance of one's own narcissism as a problem, and not as a veridical orientation toward the world, makes possible the return to mutualistic, mutually dependent, relations with others who have done so as well. It makes possible the recognition of the other as an-other. It was from this recognition, and the attendant message of limitation and vulnerability, that narcissism, in the beginning, seemed to offer a retreat—a retreat that the experience of hitting bottom revealed as being illusory. What we see here is the recognition that the need for others *as others,* and not just as elements of the self (Kohut 1971), gives a meaning to life that narcissism cannot give. Limitation, thus, appears not as a contradiction to meaning, but, for the human, an essential precondition (Bettleheim 1984).

Thus, to quote Kurtz again:

In some of A.A.'s more explicitly religiously inclined derivations, the confrontation with self by way of honesty about self with others that is outlined in Steps Four through Ten led to an understanding of the fundamental therapeutic dynamic of "The Answer to Addiction" as "devotion to truth." At root, Alcoholics Anonymous presented a simultaneously very modern and very ancient religious perception. The embrace of not-God-ness led easily to the acknowledgments: "Accept reality, for reality affirms you"; "Be devoted to truth, and the truth will set you free." Whether or not to capitalize "reality" or "truth" was left by A.A., with cautious strategic wisdom, to the individual believer. (185)

CONCLUSION: ALCOHOLICS ANONYMOUS AND THE RECOVERY FROM ORGANIZATIONAL DECAY

The acceptance of reality, the sense of limitation, and the mutuality that we have seen its acceptance to make possible are of course the key to Klein's (1975) concept of the depressive position. Within the depressive position, the reparative process, the process of making amends to those whom we have injured through the narcissistic demands that we have made on them,[6] provides an important basis for such hope as we may manage in the present condition of society (Hirschhorn 1988). And as part of a process of mutual affirmation with the other, it provides a rich motivational basis for doing good work.[7]

As Lapierre (1989) observes, the depressive position also offers a sound basis for the management of organizations, and one that is in perfect accord with the truth we found in the cultural management literature concerning the importance excellent organizations place on doing work. For, in the depressive position, the organization is seen very simply as *the organization of the work process,* and *management is nothing but the management of the work process.* It does not require the reduction of others to the role of supporting actors in a drama starring the manager, and therefore it makes possible real communication about work and mutual respect for doing it. It involves the mutual acceptance of limitation and does not therefore require the pretense of perfection that necessitates the denial of the self and its own realistic perceptions. I could go on like this, but for the present it may be more useful just to make one observation that would sum up all the rest: this organization would not be the manager's route to the ego ideal, and therefore it would not require the imposition of irrationality upon the work process to maintain its motivational integrity.

In terms of the present crisis of organizations, and specifically with regard to the problems of narcissistic process that are so prominent among them, there are both positive and negative consequences of the perspective of the depressive position. On the negative side is the recognition that the use of power cannot avail in "doing something" about this problem. This perspective suggests that narcissism, like alcoholism, requires a self-diagnosis before it can yield to treatment. But denial is one of its primary symptoms. This means that a cure cannot be imposed. The narcissist, like the alcoholic, must hit his or her own bottom.

What makes this frightening is that the narcissists we have in mind are those who have become addicted to the use of organizational power to maintain their sense of their own grandeur. They may not reach bottom until the use of organizational power in the service of denial has exhausted organizational power—when, in other words, organizations no longer have power because they are no longer functioning organizations. In the case of an organization like General Motors, one easily gets the feeling that, like the chorus of a Greek tragedy, one is watching powerless, in awe and horror, as the tragic flaw plays its way out to inevitable and final catastrophe.

On the optimistic side, I believe one must count the gains that are being made by the society in recognizing the addiction that lies at its core and, finally, beginning to do something about it. One must see the growth of organizations like Alcoholics Anonymous as having an influence that extends beyond the physical treatment of alcoholism and toward the rebirth of a society that will be sober in a much deeper sense.

Thus, in the end, what we need to see is that hope lies in the possibility of a cultural change. In this I find myself in agreement with the champions of cultural management. Where we disagree is, of course, that they see this change taking place through the power of the powerful. Cultural change can indeed be imposed, but when it is imposed, it bears with it the narcissistic assumptions that underlie its attempted promulgation. Spiritual growth, in other words, cannot be imposed; only totalitarianism can be. The evidence from our own organizations, not to mention that from the collapse of the Communist regimes of Eastern Europe, makes it clear enough that this sort of thing does not work very well.

The lesson of Alcoholics Anonymous is that the sort of change we have in mind will not be caused *by* the powerful. Rather, if it happens, it will happen *to* the powerful in exactly the same way it happens to everybody else. And, if it happens, it will not happen quickly and once-and-for-all. Rather, like the slow growth of the recovering alcoholic, it will happen only gradually, slowly, painfully, and always partially. As they say in AA, "It took you a long time to get sick; it will take you a long time to get better."

Notes

1. THE CLOCKWORK OR THE SNAKEPIT

1. The text by Klein and Ritti (1984) is a notable exception.

2. ON THE PSYCHODYNAMICS OF ORGANIZATIONAL TOTALITARIANISM

1. Putting the matter more precisely, I might say that psychological involvement in the organization is a result of taking it as an ego ideal and that commitment is the case in which the organization is the individual's *exclusive* ego ideal. Since I am concerned to discuss the psychology and consequences of taking the organization as the ego ideal, it seems appropriate to concentrate on the "ideal case" of commitment. Nonetheless, much of what will be said here applies to cases of less exclusive psychological involvement as well. Some of the totalitarian processes described in this chapter serve strongly to strengthen the importance of the organization as ego ideal by rendering other involvements untenable. Other circumstances that lead to exclusive commitment will be discussed in the next chapter.
2. I have elsewhere (1983b) developed a psychodynamic interpretation of Maslow's hierarchy.
3. Note the connection between this depth dimension and Schein's (1980) concept of organizational centrality.
4. For a further discussion of the psychodynamics of hierarchy, see Schwartz (1987).
5. What has been said with regard to cognitive bias could have been said as well in terms of the theory of retrospective sense-making (Weick 1969). Here, a distinction would be noted between the leader, whose retrospective justifications would be taken as valid, and followers, who would have to adapt to the retrospective sense of the leader while being subject to having the sense of their own actions determined for them by the leader. Alternatively, the differentiation could have been drawn in terms of Argyris and Schön's (1974) distinction between espoused theories and theories-in-use. In this case, the espoused theories of the leader would have to be taken by followers as being the leader's theory-in-use, while the followers' theory-in-use would always be available to be held up by the leader as differing from the acceptable espoused theories—espoused theories that, as has been noted, must be publicly declared as guiding the behavior of the leader.

4. TOTALITARIAN MANAGEMENT AND
ORGANIZATIONAL DECAY

1. I am indebted to Harry Levinson for insisting that I address this point.
2. Note the connection here with the findings of Luthans, Hodgetts, and Rosenkrantz (1988) on the unrelatedness of competence and organizational success. From the point of view of the theory of organizational decay, the further intriguing possibility presents itself that these researchers have managed to capture only a phase of the decay process. On the basis of the considerations adduced here, one would expect to find that as the organization decayed further, the correlation between competence and organizational success would become negative. In organizations of this sort, bad management drives out good.
3. It is interesting to note that the isolation of management from criticism takes place outside of the corporation as well. Thus, in the 28 August 1989 issue of *Fortune* magazine, an article by Julie Connelly called "The CEO's Second Wife" details what happens to the first:

   > As their husbands rise in the corporation, first wives may become convinced that power is corrupting the presumably wholesome lads they married. "They become self-appointed critics and consciences," says Manhattan psychiatrist Clifford Sager, who specializes in marital therapy. "They try to cut their husbands down to size." (55)

4. In retrospect, it seems clear enough to me that a good many of the processes described in this work are those discussed by Janis (1982). The advantage of the present approach is that it provides psychodynamic grounding for the concept of groupthink and shows the working of these processes in a number of organizational dimensions, rather than just decision-making.
5. The contrast between the benign world of the role performance and the malevolent world of the performers is illustrated in Terkel's (1974) interview with Larry Ross, a former president of a conglomerate. Thus:

   > You walk down the corridor and everybody bows and says, "Good morning, Mr. Ross. How are you today?" As you go up the line, the executives will say, "How is Mrs. Ross?" Until you get to the higher executives. They'll say, "How is Nancy?" Here you socialize, you know each other. Everybody plays the game. (411)

   But:

   > As he struggles in this jungle, every position he's in, he's terribly lonely. He can't confide and talk with the guy working under him. He can't confide and talk to the man he's working for. To give vent to his feelings, his fears, and his insecurities he'd expose himself. This goes all the way up the line until he gets to be president. The president *really* doesn't have anybody to talk to, because the vice presidents are waiting for him to die or make a mistake and get knocked off so they can get his job. (408)

6. Actually, what we have here is a form of "retreat from language" of the type that concerned John R. Searle (1969: 198) when he wrote:

The retreat from the committed use of words ultimately must involve a retreat from language itself, for speaking a language. . . . consists of performing speech acts according to rules, and there is no separating those speech acts from the commitments which form essential aspects of them. (Cited in Hummel 1987)

Also see Hummel's interesting discussion of the separation of language from meaning in bureaucracy.

7. DeLorean's account here is in accordance with Mintzberg's (1973) observations of managerial work. It is tempting to speculate that much of what Mintzberg was observing was not managerial work, as such, but rather a decadent form of it.

8. Kets de Vries and Miller's (1984) discussion of "utopian culture" is related.

9. The word around Detroit, as I write this, is that the Saturn will have nothing special to recommend it. Of course, as Keller (1989) notes, if people do not buy the Saturn, the whole "revolutionary" process that has such sales as its end will be rendered meaningless.

5. ORGANIZATIONAL DISASTER AND ORGANIZATIONAL DECAY

1. It is absolutely essential that the reader understand that we are not engaged in "20-20 hindsight" here, but that NASA management was making errors that a reasonable person would not have made *given the information available at the time.* A reading of chapter 6 of volume 1 of the Rogers Commission report will, I believe, convince anybody of this, but it may be useful to give some idea of the sky-blue–heaven thinking that NASA management was using in employing such concepts as "safety margin." I quote here from the Rogers Commission report:

> From the beginning, Thiokol had suspected the putty was a contributing factor in O-ring erosion, even after STS-2. In April 1983, Thiokol reported on tests conducted to study the behavior of the joint putty. One conclusion of the report was that the STS-2 erosion was probably caused by blow holes in the putty, which allowed a jet of hot gas to focus on the primary O-ring. Thiokol discovered the focused jet ate away or "impinged" on portions of the O-ring. Thiokol calculated that the maximum possible impingement erosion was .090 inch, and that lab test proved that an O-ring would seal at 3,000 psi when erosion of .095 was simulated. This "safety margin" was the basis for approving Shuttle flights while accepting the possibility of O-ring erosion. (133)

2. Readers will be aided in coming to a proper appreciation of NASA management by knowing that seven out of nine flights during 1985 were found to have had erosion and that six of them had blow-by (RC 1986: 130–31).

3. An earlier game that Feynman made up for himself won him the Nobel Prize.

4. In response to Feynman's skepticism, Lovingood offered: "Sir, I'll be glad to send you the document that contains this estimate, so you can understand it." Referring back to the previous section on how the organization's self-

idealization distorts its view of reality, it is worthwhile to quote Feynman's comment on what followed:

> Later, Mr. Lovingood sent me that report. It said things like "The probability of mission success is necessarily very close to 1.0"—does that mean it *is* close to 1.0, or it *ought to be* close to 1.0?—and "Historically, this high degree of mission success has given rise to a difference in philosophy between unmanned and manned space flight programs; i.e. numerical probability versus engineering judgment." As far as I can tell, "engineering judgment" means they're just going to make up numbers! The probability of an engine-blade failure was given as a universal constant, as if all blades were exactly the same, under the same conditions. The whole paper was quantifying everything. Just about every nut and bolt was in there: "The chance that a HPHTP pipe will burst is 10^{-7}." You can't estimate things like that; a probability of 1 in 10,000,000 is almost impossible to estimate. It was clear that the numbers for each part of the engine were chosen so that when you add everything together you get 1 in 100,000. (183n)

6. ON THE PSYCHODYNAMICS OF ORGANIZATIONAL DISASTER

1. Strictly speaking, they retained their professional standards as part of their superego—the set of obligations understood as expressing the conditions for the attainment of the ego ideal. This distinction will be explored further in the next chapter.
2. Pauchant and Mitroff (1988) reported the results of a study that found that organizations with nonnarcissistic cultures had integrated crisis management programs, while organizations with narcissistic cultures did not.

7. THE SYMBOL OF THE SPACE SHUTTLE AND THE AMERICAN DREAM

1. Compare here Max Weber's *The Protestant Ethic and the Spirit of Capitalism* (New York: Scribner's 1958).

8. CONCLUSION: ADDICTION AND RECOVERY

1. Elsewhere (Weick 1977), I have noted that "reality is a metaphor" . . .

> By that, I meant that talk about "a reality" is simply one way that people try to make sense out of the stream of experience that flows by them. To say that there is a reality, an environment, and then to search for and discover underlying patterns in those superimposed structures is one way to make sense of that stream. But the tenuousness of this process, as well as the actor's central role in its execution, are captured only if we remain attentive to reality *as* metaphor. . . .

And he adds:

> Literally, to enact an environment can mean to "create the appearance of an

environment" or to "simulate an environment for the sake of representation." . . .
Members act as if they have environments, create the appearance of environments, or
simulate environments for the sake of getting on with their business. These organizing
acts are acts of invention rather than acts of discovery, they involve a superimposed
order rather than an underlying order, and they are based on the assumption that
cognition follows the trail of action. (Weick 1977: 278)

The fact is that Weick denies the existence of an external world:

While the categories external/internal or outside/inside exist logically, they do not
exist empirically. The "outside" or "external" world cannot be known. There is no
methodological process by which one can confirm the existence of an object independent of the confirmatory process involving oneself. *The outside is a void, there is only
the inside.* A person's world, the inside or internal view is all that can be known. The
rest can only be the object of speculation. (273, emphasis added)

Weick is evidently not aware that in denying a referent to the concept
outer he abolishes the meaning of the distinction *inner/outer* and thereby
also loses the meaningfulness of *inner*. What we are left with, of course, is
the predifferentiated matrix of infant/mother, self/other with which we are
familiar.

2. The actual methodology goes like this: first, you get people to act the way
you want them to; Then, you manage the meaning they place upon their
action so that they come to interpret it the way you want them to. This is
from Peters and Waterman (1982):

only if you get people *acting*, even in small ways, the way you want them to, will they
come to believe in what they're doing. Moreover, the process of enlistment is enhanced by explicit *management* of the after-the-act labeling process. (74)

And:

The role of the leader, then, is one of orchestrator and labeler: taking what can be
gotten in the way of action and shaping it—generally after the fact—into lasting
commitment to a new strategic direction. In short, he makes meanings. (75)

The problem with this approach is not merely that it applies to adults a
model of consciousness that properly pertains to fetuses and infants. The
main problem goes much deeper.

In one sense, of course, Weick is quite correct. One cannot prove the
existence of an external world ("Prove it to whom?" one might ask.) But
this says less about the existence of an external world than it does about the
nature of proof. It says that if the existence of the external world (or
anything else) does not go into the proof as a premise, it cannot emerge as a
conclusion. But there is no news in this, and has not been since the Greeks
began their explorations into the nature of logic.

What is frightening is the way such skepticism about the simplest facts
of existence leads to the demand for total, irrational commitment to the
most elaborate fabrications in the totalitarian system. Evidently, when
experience has been delegitimated, for that is what we are talking about

here, the only criterion of truth becomes conformity to the official doctrine. And the determination of the content of this doctrine comes to be decided by pure, unconstrained power—power which recognizes no necessity to justify itself. Consider cultural management in the context of this from George Orwell's *1984*:

> In the end the Party would announce that two and two made five, and you would have to believe it. It was inevitable that they should make that claim sooner or later: the logic of their position demanded it. Not merely the validity of experience, but the very existence of external reality was tacitly denied by their philosophy. The heresy of heresies was common sense. And what was terrifying was not that they would kill you for thinking otherwise, but that they might be right. For, after all, how do we know that two and two make four? Or that the force of gravity works? Or that the past is unchangeable? If both the past and the external world exist only in the mind, and if the mind is controllable—what then? (69)

3. For an earlier attempt to answer this question see Schwartz (1985).
4. For a similar analysis, see Schaef and Fassel (1988).
5. "Religion is for people who don't want to go to hell. Spirituality is for people who have been to hell and don't want to go back," says Don C.
6. Reparation is an integral part of the AA program. It is referred to most specifically in the eighth and ninth steps: "Made a list of all persons we had harmed, and became willing to make amends to them all" and "Made direct amends to such people wherever possible, except when to do so would injure them or others."
7. I have written on the subject of reparation as a psychology of work in an unpublished paper (1984). Larry Hirschhorn (1988) makes reparation a major element of his theory of postindustrial culture. In contrast to his approach, I see reparation as involving an attempt to compensate for real damage to real others and therefore as taking place within the psychodynamics of guilt. He seems to see it as the reconstruction of an illusion, taking place within the psychodynamics of shame. I have also discussed work within the context of the superego (Schwartz, 1983a, 1983b), which I see as being a specific structure within the depressive position.

Actually, I think there is an emerging view among psychoanalytically oriented writers on organizations that the classic superego has become outmoded. Hirschhorn, who perhaps best represents this view, notes that the superego represents punishing voices from the past; but punishing voices from the past can no longer serve our purposes in the complex and rapidly changing present. The unconscious guilt that the Freudian superego represents must give way before conscious, responsible choice between the better and the worse. Repression is no longer viable as a means of directing ourselves. We must, as he contends, have our affects present to us in our work.

References

Alford, C. F. 1990. The organization of evil. *Political Psychology* 11(1):5–27.

Arendt, H. 1966. *The origins of totalitarianism.* New York: Harcourt, Brace and World.

Argyris, C. 1957. *Personality and organization: The conflict between the system and the individual.* New York: Harper and Row.

———. 1964. *Integrating the individual and the organization.* New York: Wiley.

———. 1985. *Strategy, change, and defensive routines.* Boston: Pitman.

———, and D. A. Schön. 1974. *Theory in practice.* San Francisco: Jossey-Bass.

Baum, H. S. 1987. *The invisible bureaucracy: The unconscious in organizational problem solving.* New York: Oxford University Press.

Becker, E. 1971. *The birth and death of meaning.* 2d ed. New York: Free Press.

———. 1973. *The denial of death.* New York: Free Press.

———. 1975. *Escape from evil.* New York: Free Press.

Bettleheim, B. 1984. *Freud and man's soul.* New York: Vintage.

Burns, J. M. 1978. *Leadership.* New York: Harper and Row.

Chasseguet-Smirgel, J. 1985. *The ego ideal: A psychoanalytic essay on the malady of the ideal.* Translated by P. Barrows. New York: Norton.

———. 1986. *Sexuality and mind: The role of the father and the mother in the psyche.* New York: New York University Press.

Culbert, S. A., and J. J. McDonough. 1980. *The invisible war: Pursuing self-interests at work.* New York: Wiley.

Cummings, L. L. 1983. The logics of management. *Academy of Management Review* 8(4):532–38.

Deal, T. E. and A. A. Kennedy. 1982. *Corporate cultures: The rites and rituals of corporate life.* Reading, Mass.: Addison-Wesley

Denhardt, R. D. 1981. *In the shadow of organization.* Lawrence, Kans.: Regents Press of Kansas.

Diamond, M. 1984. Bureaucracy as externalized self-system: A view from the psychological interior. *Administration and Society* 16(2):195–214.

Festinger, L., H. W. Riecken, and S. Schacter. 1956. *When prophecy fails.* Minneapolis: University of Minnesota Press.

Feynman, R. P. 1989. *"What do you care about what other people think?": Further adventures of a curious character.* New York: Bantam Books.

Freud, S. 1938. *Totem and taboo.* In *The basic writings of Sigmund Freud,* translated and edited by A. A. Brill. New York: Modern Library.

———. 1955a. *Group psychology and the analysis of the ego.* Standard edition, vol. 18. London: Hogarth Press.

Freud, S. 1955b. *Beyond the pleasure principle.* Standard edition, vol. 18. London: Hogarth Press.

——. 1957. *On narcissism: An introduction.* Standard edition, vol. 14. London: Hogarth Press.

——. 1961. *Civilization and its discontents.* Standard edition, vol. 21. London: Hogarth Press.

Goffman, E. 1959. *The presentation of self in everyday life.* New York: Doubleday, Anchor.

Geertz, C. 1973. *The interpretation of cultures.* New York: Basic Books.

Hackman, J. R., G. Oldham, R. Janson, and K. Purdy. 1975. A new strategy of job enrichment. *California Management Review* 17:57–71.

Halberstam, D. 1986. *The reckoning.* New York: William Morrow.

Hirschhorn, L. 1988. *The workplace within: Psychodynamics of organizational life.* Cambridge, MIT Press.

Hohler, R. T. 1986. *"I touch the future . . .": The story of Christa McAuliffe.* New York: Random House.

Horney, K. 1950. *Neurosis and human growth.* New York: Norton.

Hummel, R. P. 1987. *The bureaucratic experience.* 3d ed. New York: St. Martin's Press

Ingrassia, P., and J. B. White. 1989. Losing the race: With its market share sliding, GM scrambles to avoid a calamity. *Wall Street Journal,* 14 December.

Janis, I. I. 1982. *Groupthink.* 2d ed. Boston: Houghton Mifflin.

Katz, D., and R. L. Kahn. 1966. *The social psychology of organizations.* New York: Wiley.

Keller, M. 1989. *Rude awakening: The rise, fall, and struggle for recovery of General Motors.* New York: William Morrow.

Kernberg, O. 1975. *Borderline conditions and pathological narcissism.* New York: Jason Aronson.

Kets de Vries, M. F. R., and D. Miller. 1984. *The neurotic organization.* San Francisco: Jossey-Bass.

Klein, Melanie. 1975. A contribution to the psychogenesis of manic-depressive states. In *Love, guilt, and reparation, and other works, 1921–1945.* London: Hogarth Press.

Klein, S. M., and R. R. Ritti. 1984. *Understanding organizational behavior.* 2d ed. Boston: Kent.

Kohut, H. 1971. *The analysis of the self.* New York: International Universities Press.

Kurtz, E. 1979. *Not-God: The history of alcoholics anonymous.* Center City, Minn.: Hazelden.

Lapierre, L. 1989. Mourning, potency, and power in management. *Human Resource Management,* 28(2):177–89.

Lasch, C. 1979. *The culture of narcissism.* New York: Warner.

——. 1984. *The minimal self.* New York: Norton.

Levinson, D. J. 1978. *The seasons of a man's life.* New York: Knopf.

Lichtenstein, H. 1977. *The dilemma of human identity*. New York: Jason Aronson.

Likert, R. 1961. *New patterns of management*. New York: McGraw-Hill.

Luthans, F., R. M. Hodgetts, and S. A. Rosenkrantz. 1988. *Real managers*. Cambridge, Mass.: Ballinger.

March, J. G., and H. A. Simon. 1958. *Organizations*. New York: Wiley.

Maslow, A. H. 1970. *Motivation and personality*. 2d ed. New York: Harper and Row.

McGregor, D. 1960. *The human side of enterprise*. New York: McGraw-Hill.

McGill, M. E. 1988. *American Business and the quick fix*. New York: Henry Holt.

Mead, G. H. 1934. *Mind, self, and society*. Chicago: University of Chicago Press.

Milgram, S. 1963. Behavioural study of obedience. *Journal of Abnormal and Social Psychology* 67:371–78.

Mintzberg, H. 1973. *The nature of managerial work*. New York: Harper and Row.

Mowday, R. T., L. W. Porter, and R. M. Steers. 1982. *Employee-organization linkages*. New York: Academic Press.

Murray, B. 1986. Interview on "This Week With David Brinkley." ABC Television, 8 June.

Nader, R., and W. Taylor. 1986. *The big boys: Power and position in American business*. New York: Pantheon.

Orwell, G. 1949. *1984*. New York: Harcourt, Brace, Jovanovich.

Parsons, T. 1954. An analytical approach to the theory of social stratification. In *Essays in sociological theory*. Rev. ed. New York: Free Press.

Pauchant, T., and I. Mitroff. 1988. Crisis-prone versus crisis-avoiding organizations: Is your company's culture its own worst enemy in creating crises? Working paper, Laval University.

Peters, Thomas J., and R. H. Waterman. 1982. *In search of excellence: Lessons from America's best-run companies*. New York: Harper and Row.

Piers, G., and Singer, M. B. 1953. *Shame and guilt*. Springfield, Ill.: Charles C. Thomas.

Pfeffer, J. 1981. *Power in organizations*. Marshfield, Mass.: Pitman.

Rogers, W. P. 1986. *Report of the presidential commission on the space shuttle Challenger accident*. Washington, D.C.: United States Government Printing Office.

Sartre, J. 1953. *Being and nothingness*. New York: Philosophical Library.

Schaef, A. W., and D. Fassel. 1988. *The addictive organization*. New York: Harper and Row.

Schein, E. H. 1980. *Organizational psychology*. 3d ed. Englewood Cliffs, N.J.: Prentice Hall.

———. 1983. Organizational socialization and the profession of management. In *Psychological foundation of organization behavior*. 2d ed., edited by Barry M. Staw. Glenview, Ill.: Scott, Foresman.

Schwartz, H. S. 1982. Job involvement as obsession compulsion. *Academy of Management Review* 7(3):429–32.

———. 1983a. A theory of deontic work motivation. *Journal of Applied Behavioral Science* 19(2):203–14.

———. 1983b. Maslow and the hierarchical enactment of organizational reality. *Human Relations* 36(10):933–56.

———. 1984. Two psychologies of work. Paper presented at the International Society of Political Psychology meetings, June 1984, Toronto.

———. 1985. The usefulness of myth and the myth of usefulness: A dilemma for the applied organizational scientist. *Journal of Management* 11(1):31–42.

———. 1987. Rousseau's *Discourse on inequality* revisited: Psychology of work at the public esteem stage of Maslow's hierarchy." *International Journal of Management* 4(2):180–93.

Shorris, E. 1981. *The oppressed middle: Politics of middle management/Scenes from corporate life.* Garden City, N.Y.: Doubleday, Anchor.

Sievers, B. 1986. Beyond the surrogate of motivation. *Organization Studies* 7(4):335–51.

Starbuck, W. H., and F. J. Milliken. 1988. Challenger: Fine-tuning the odds until somethings breaks." *Journal of Management Studies* 25(4):319–40.

Staw, B. M. 1980. Rationality and justification in organization life. In *Research in organizational behavior*, vol. 2, edited by B. M. Staw and L. L. Cummings, 45–80. Greenwich, Conn.: JAI Press.

Terkel, S. 1974. *Working.* New York: Pantheon.

Trento, J. J. 1987. *Prescription for disaster: From the glory of Apollo to the betrayal of the shuttle.* New York: Crown.

Wanous, J. P. 1975. Tell it like it is at realistic job previews. *Personnel* (July–August).

Weick, K. E. 1977. Enactment processes in organizations. In *New directions in organizational behavior*, edited by B. M. Staw and G. R. Salancik. Chicago: St. Clair Press.

———. 1969. *The social psychology of organizing.* Reading, Mass.: Addison-Wesley.

———. 1988. Organizational culture as a source of high reliability." in *Organizations close-up: A book of readings.* 6th ed., edited by J. L. Gibson, J. M. Ivancevich, and J. H. Donnelly, Jr.. Plano, Tex.: Business Publications.

Weiner, B., I. Frieze, A. Kulka, L. Reed, S. Rest, and R. M. Rosenbaum. 1971. *Perceiving the causes of success and failure.* Morristown, N.J.: General Learning Press.

Wolfe, T. 1979. *The right stuff.* New York: Farrar, Straus and Giroux.

Wright, J. P. 1979. *On a clear day you can see General Motors: John Z. De Lorean's look inside the automotive giant.* New York: Avon.

Index